St. Augustine Academy Press

About **Mother Mary St. Peter:**

Born Jane Lansdowne in England in 1841, from an early age she was educated by the Dominican Sisters in Stone, Staffordshire. She then joined the Society of the Holy Child Jesus, which was still in its infancy, having been founded by Cornelia Connelly in 1846. She was admitted as a postulant in 1862, professed her vows in 1864, and was a well-beloved teacher for many years in the Convent schools. In 1876 she was chosen as Prefect for a new school in Paris, but to her great disappointment, she was unable to take the post, and instead was sent in 1885 to America, where she taught in Nebraska, Minnesota and Wyoming before returning to the motherhouse in Sharon Hill, Pennsylvania in 1897. Here she took up writing as a way of helping to raise money for building the chapel there. "Isn't God good to let me work on these little books?" she once said. "I always wanted to write books on Christian Doctrine and now at the end He is graciously allowing it." She kept up her work until the day she died, writing over a dozen books and plays, the last of which had to be finished by a fellow sister upon her death in 1906.

About ***The Queen's Festivals:***

"This book is written primarily for children, with the object of making them understand, first, what is meant by festivals in general, and secondly, why we celebrate the special feasts of the Blessed Virgin in particular. These festivals are divided into three classes: the Queen's anniversaries, the Queen's titles, and, lastly, the Queen's Sundays, closing with a devout consideration of the Queen's month—May. The author understands how to bring truths home to the childish heart and mind. [Her] style cannot fail to be fascinating and instructive to the little ones, but even adults will find the book unusually instructive, clear and unctuous." —The Rosary Magazine, June 1907.

MARY THE QUEEN

THE SEAT OF WISDOM SERIES

The Queen's Festivals

An Explanation of the Feasts of the Blessed Virgin Mary

by
MOTHER MARY ST. PETER
of the Society of the Holy Child Jesus

edited by
LISA BERGMAN
and
DAVID BRANDT

2016
ST. AUGUSTINE ACADEMY PRESS
HOMER GLEN, ILLINOIS

This book is newly typeset based on
the edition published in 1907 by Benziger Brothers.

The text has been modified in places in order to render it more
accessible to modern readers; this was done with great care and
sensitivity toward the age of the material, in order to maintain
respect for the era in which it was written, as well as to
preserve the original writer's voice.
Though the wording has been thus modified,
the content itself has been changed only as follows:
1. To add the story of Our Lady of Fatima.
2. To add other minor details of interest to certain chapters.
3. To improve the structure and flow of difficult-to-follow portions.

All scripture quotations taken from the Douay-Rheims Bible.

Nihil obstat:
    Remigius Lafort, S.T.L.,
        Censor Librorum

Imprimatur:
    ✠ John M. Farley,
        Archbishop of New York

New York, December 9, 1906.

This book was originally published by Benziger Brothers in 1907.
This edited and annotated edition ©2016
by St. Augustine Academy Press.
Editing and Notes by Lisa Bergman and David Brandt.

ISBN: 978-1-936639-64-9
Library of Congress Control Number: 2016958042

Unless otherwise noted, all illustrations in this book,
including the cover, are public domain images.

Contents

PREFACE   VII

Part I: Introduction

   I. Something About Festivals   1
   II. Something About Liturgy   7
   III. Something About the Liturgy of the Mass   13

Part II: The Queen's Anniversaries

   IV. The Immaculate Conception   23
   V. The Nativity of the Blessed Virgin   31
   VI. Feast of the Holy Name of Mary   35
   VII. The Presentation   39
   VIII. The Espousals   43
   IX. The Annunciation   47
   X. The Visitation   53
   XI. The Expectation   59
   XII. The Purification   63
   XIII. The Assumption   69

Part III: Festivals of the Queen's Titles

   XIII. Our Lady Help of Christians   79
   XIV. Our Lady of Mount Carmel   83
   XV. The Blessed Virgin Mary ad Nives   89
   XVI. The Blessed Virgin Mary of Mercy   95
   XVII. Our Lady of Lourdes   99
   XVIII. Our Lady of Good Counsel   105
   XIX. Our Lady of Perpetual Succour   111
   XX. Our Lady of Fatima   117

Part IV: The Queen's Sundays

XXI.	The Feast of the Holy Name of Mary	127
XXII.	The Feast of the Seven Dolors	131
XXIII.	Feast of the Holy Rosary	135
XXIV.	The Queen's Month	139

Preface

HOSE who are familiar with the first book in the Seat of Wisdom series, *Mary the Queen*, are already aware of the history behind the rebirth of these books by Mother Mary St. Peter. For those who are not, I would direct you to the preface written for that book to explain how we discovered her work and the methodology we have used to prepare these newly reprinted versions.

In this volume, we were presented with a new challenge: some of the subjects within, especially the Mass and the ranking of feasts, used terminology and descriptions that are no longer used or are foreign to modern Catholics. Thus while we continued to exercise great care in materially altering as little as possible, there were places where our barebones editing had to be eschewed in favor of crafting explanations that were more straightforward and accessible to those unfamiliar with these details. At times we also chose to add minor details that Mother St. Peter had omitted in the interest of brevity; where further illustration enriched the narrative we did not hesitate to expand these slightly.

Our biggest struggle, however, was deciding how much to update and how much to respect the age of the material. Each festival throughout this book is classified according to its ranking at the time (i.e. Double, Semidouble, etc.) and we strongly considered updating these to use more recent terminology. Unfortunately, as this terminology has changed more than once in the past 100 years, and as some of these feasts have been moved or supplanted in the Calendar since this book was written, we found it impossible to be consistent. Moreover, to fully update certain portions, like the description of the Mass, would have been too far unfaithful to the original, as it would have required wholesale rewriting of entire pages. We therefore encourage the reader to seek more information on each feast and its current ranking if desired.

One thing we could not bear to omit, however, was the story of Our Lady of Fatima. As this book predates the apparitions themselves, of course it could not have been included among the stories of Our Lady's Festivals within. But while many other apparitions—including Our Lady of Guadalupe and Our Lady of LaSalette—could easily have been included as well, we could neither expand the book so greatly as to include all the approved apparitions, nor allow so important a story as that which took place at Fatima to be overlooked. Thus we have done our best to add that story in a style as close as we could manage to the author's own.

We trust that *The Queen's Festivals* will greatly expand the reader's knowledge of Our Lady and encourage further exploration, as there is more to be learned on this subject than could possibly be contained in one—or two—books.

Yours in Christ,
Lisa Bergman
St. Augustine Academy Press
Feast of Christ the King, 2016

Part I

Introduction

Dignare me laudare te, Virgo sacrata:
Da mihi virtutem contra hostes tuos.

Vidi per somnium quasi solem et lunam. Gen. 37, 9.

Regina Saba dedit regi centum viginti tal. III Reg. 10.

THE QUEEN'S FESTIVALS

Chapter I

Something About Festivals

A GOOD priest who has much to do with children and knows well what they need looked through a little life of the Blessed Mother called "Mary the Queen" and then said, "There should be more about the Queen's Festivals." But it happened that no space was left in that book for "more about the Queen's Festivals," and on such a subject there is really a great deal to be said. After all, there are a great many stories to tell, too, and everybody—that is, every right-minded body—likes stories. So the only thing to be done under the circumstances was to give the Festivals a little book of their own, and therein tell the children who love their Mother in heaven as much as we can about those Festivals—and the stories too.

First of all, let us begin at the beginning and find out what a feast of Our Lady, a "Queen's Festival," really is. Perhaps you think that very unnecessary, as you already know quite well, and no doubt some of you do. Still, people sometimes make mistakes and imagine that they know a great deal more than they do.

A number of children were once asked, "What is a holiday?" A tiny girl—she was very tiny—answered at once, "I know; it's talking all day and nuts for supper." She looked round in great astonishment when everybody laughed.

Another little girl was promised a party for her birthday. When the day came, her companions arrived at three in the afternoon, and she was told to show them her toys and take them to play in the garden, which she did. But Helen had seen a long table prettily decorated with pink roses, and had caught a glimpse of a cake covered with icing and having five pink candles and somebody's name on the top. She could not give her whole mind to the games. So presently she slipped away from the other small people and whispered to her aunt, "When will the party begin, Auntie?"

To her, you see, a party meant cake and ice cream.

And once upon a time some children who went to school in a very poor quarter of a very large city wanted to make Our Lady's altar as beautiful as they could to do honor to the "Feast" of the Patron Saint of the Sister who taught them. So the elders among them went round exhorting their companions to bring pennies for "our Sister's feast." Their pennies were few, poor little souls, but they brought them readily, and "our Sister," who had not lived long among the very poor of a great city, was both puzzled and amazed when one of her youngest pupils whispered, "Oh, Sister, you'll have hot beef and pudding to-morrow! I brought twopence for you."

Hot beef and pudding was her idea of a feast—and she got one seldom enough, I'm afraid.

Now, each of those children was a little right, and they were all a good deal wrong in their definitions; and perhaps that is just what you may be in your notions of "festivals," or the Queen's Days.

The feasts—more correctly called the festivals of Our Lady—are days which have been set aside by the Church to be celebrated in her honor just as in your family you celebrate the anniversary of your parents' wedding, and that of your own birthday; or as the people generally celebrate Washington's and Lincoln's birthdays in honor of those two presidents; the Fourth of July in commemoration of the Declaration of Independence of their country; and Thanksgiving Day in memory of the first harvest gathered in New England by the Pilgrim Fathers. These are called National Festivals.

As I told you, the Queen's Festivals have been set aside by the Church, who tells us what to do in all matters connected with faith and morals, and the Church teaches us why each festival has been appointed, and in what manner it is to be observed.

We hear a great deal in these days about long hours and overwork, and laboring people are always asking for less work and more pay. When Mother Church was allowed to manage her own affairs, and all Christians acknowledged her as their Mother, she looked after the welfare of her children as a good mother should. She knows that "All work and no play makes Jack a dull boy," quite as well as Jack knows it himself, and took care that playtime should be provided for him.

But if she was anxious that her children should not be overworked, she was far more desirous that they should get to heaven; so instead of making holidays in memory of a king or president, or the Declaration of Independence, and arranging that her playdays should be celebrated by the giving of Martha Washington Receptions, setting off fireworks, and eating turkey and mince pies, Mother Church invited her merrymakers to keep festivals in honor of Our Lord, His Blessed Mother, and the saints. They were to have the turkey and the fireworks, and as much innocent fun as they could get—but she bade them go to holy Mass first, and to devote a portion besides of their playdays to the more especial service of God.

As there were many of these days set aside in the first ages, and the number increased as time went on, not all of them were kept as full holidays, nor were the faithful actually commanded to hear Mass on every one.

In the very early ages, indeed, a command was not needed, for people were more fervent then than now; and not only very holy persons, but even ordinary Christians had the good habit of going to Mass every day, whether it was a festival or not.

In course of time devotion cooled, and then it became necessary to say that on the very great festivals Mass must be heard; also that no unnecessary servile work may be done. These days were to be kept just like Sundays, and were called Holy Days of Obligation. On other less important festivals, the faithful were not *commanded* but *advised* to be present at holy Mass, and such days were called Days of Devotion.

Now I must tell you that not only did the Church in the earlier ages provide days of rest and amusement, but she also provided amusement and rest. On the mornings of festivals there was the High Mass with grand music and singing, and a sermon; sometimes a good long sermon too. Few persons knew how to read back then, and those who could read found it difficult to obtain books, for printing was not invented until the fifteenth century, and thus everything had to be written and copied by hand. Of course such books cost a very great deal of money, so people who were not rich enough to buy them were glad to learn from those who had access to books and were ready to teach. For that reason, among others, they liked sermons.

Then there were beautiful stained-glass windows in the churches, and large paintings on the walls, and these served the purposes of books, and as a recreation for the people too, for in their own homes none but the very wealthy saw really beautiful things.

Then "ballads and lays," as they were called—stories in verse that were learned by heart and sung, sometimes to the music of the harp—were sung or recited, and people learned stories, whether in prose or verse, much as you do now. They learned much of their religion in this way, and a very pleasant way it was. There are some old Christmas carols, and some good imitations of them, in which the whole history and doctrine of the Nativity of Our Lord are set forth to music, as in "Listen, Lordings, Unto Me" and "A Virgin Unspotted":

> A Virgin unspotted, the prophet foretold,
> Should bring forth a Savior, which now we behold.
> To be our Redeemer from death, hell and sin,
> Which Adam's transgression had wrapped us in.
>
> > Aye and therefore be merry, set sorrow aside,
> > Christ Jesus, our Savior, was born on this tide.

(Through many more verses the full story is told; perhaps some time you might wish to read the rest.)

Sometimes even, on particularly grand feasts or on special occasions, a great stage was built quite near the church, and on this stage persons who had been taught by the priests or the monks performed plays representing scenes from the life of Our Lord or the history of some saint. Such dramas were called Miracle Plays, and a few are still acted at times in some of the German and Tyrolean villages. The Passion Play of Oberammergau is one.

And now I think you will understand that the festivals established by the Church fulfilled many useful purposes, every one of which was intended to promote the good of souls and the honor and glory of God.

Chapter II

Something About Liturgy

ERHAPS the coming chapter will be a little more difficult to understand than the last, because it will be about some things that you may never have thought of or even heard of before. Still, it will be easier than the Alphabet or the Multiplication Table, and you have certainly mastered these.

Did you ever hear of the Liturgy of the Church? No? Well, let's try to learn just a little bit about it now; and when you are older, you will no doubt add to your knowledge of this subject, which many wise and holy people have found to be worthy of long study.

You know already that the Church has a language of her own. This language is called Latin, because it was first used in a kingdom of ancient Italy named *Latium*. It was adopted by the early Romans and was spoken, or at least understood, nearly all over the civilized world at the time of Our Lord and His Apostles. This is because the Romans who lived in Italy and took their name from their capital city, Rome, were a warlike and masterful people. They liked to be at the head of everything and to rule everybody; so they made war on all the states and kingdoms in Europe and conquered nearly all of them. They made themselves masters of the great provinces in the west of Asia, and of Egypt and the north of Africa; and wherever they went, they compelled the people whom they conquered to speak the Latin tongue, and it was taught in all the schools. Thus it became as nearly as possible a *universal* language—that is, a language that is understood and spoken throughout the civilized world.

It is true that many fine books were written in Greek, which was called the language of literature, and Greek was understood by learned persons. But Latin was understood and spoken by the unlearned as well; and it had its fine books too. If your elder brothers or sisters study Homer and Sophocles, they will likely have studied Virgil and Horace also. Moreover, they probably studied these *first*, for Latin is less difficult to master than Greek.

Now, the Apostles were told by Our Lord to go forth and teach all nations; and as all who adopted the faith had to know their prayers, the wisest plan was to compose those prayers in a language that the greater number could most easily learn and understand. For this reason the prayers of the Church were composed in Latin.

You know that the Church of Christ has four marks by which she is distinguished from all sects or other religions. The first of these is, "She is One." Another is, "She is Catholic, or Universal." Because she is One, and because she is Catholic, or Universal, she offers the same sacrifice and makes use of the same prayers all over the world wherever her children are found. And her prayers are still written and read in Latin, for although this has become what is called a *dead* language—that is, it is no longer spoken by any particular nation or people—nearly all the languages now in use are formed upon it, more or less, and it is still taught in all the good schools of all countries where the Christian religion is practiced.

The Church uses a great many *set forms of prayers,* by which we mean certain prayers which are to be used on certain occasions, and which may not be changed or put aside to suit any one's taste or convenience. There are set forms of prayers appointed for holy Mass, for the administration of the Sacraments, for public processions of the Blessed Sacrament, and for many other ceremonies and occasions. And these set forms of prayer, about which the Church has laid down laws as to when and how and where they are to be used, make up the *Liturgy* of the Church.

Aside from the Mass, there is one portion of the Liturgy which is very important, as well as very beautiful, and it is called the *Divine Office.* It consists of the Psalms of David and Lessons taken from the writings of the Fathers of the Church, which are arranged together with prayers, hymns, and antiphons, and these are to be recited at certain times of the day. All priests and the members of some Religious Orders pray this Office every day, but the only part of it you are likely to know anything about is the Sunday Vespers, which are still recited in many churches on Sunday afternoons or evenings.

Had you lived eight or nine hundred years ago, you might have also known about Matins, the very first part of the Divine Office, which is said or sung in some convents and monasteries either at midnight or at three or four o'clock in the morning. In those far-off times little boys and girls were sent to be educated by Religious, and they wore little habits and attended services in church with the grown-ups. They could have explained easily enough what you, perhaps, are wondering about. For instance, after having been present at Matins on any festival, they could have told you whether that festival was a very important one or whether it were only one of lower degree. And this is how they would have found out.

I told you that the Divine Office is made up largely of Psalms. Well, whenever Matins or Lauds are said in the morning, and likewise during Vespers in the evening, those psalms are recited in a very particular way. At the end of every Psalm, a verse called an *antiphon* is always sung or said, and a word or two of this same antiphon is said at the beginning of that same Psalm.

But on a great feast the *whole* antiphon is sung both before *and* after the Psalm. For this reason such a feast is called a *Double*. It will have particular Psalms of its own at Vespers, in place of those that are ordinarily said on that day. And these special Vespers of a Double feast will also be said on the preceding day, which is called the *Vigil* of the feast. So you see a feast of great importance has not one but two Vespers of its own.

On a feast that is ranked as a *Semi-double* the antiphons are recited normally—that is, only the few first words of the antiphon are said before each Psalm. However, as in the Double feast, the Psalms are proper—that is, they belong to the feast—and there are first and second Vespers.

On feasts ranked as *Simples*—that is, days which have no special Office—everything is recited normally: the first few words of the antiphon are said before each Psalm; the whole antiphon after each Psalm; and the Psalms are those of every day.

Now I hope with this briefest of explanations you will better understand what is meant when you see feasts marked "Double," "Semi-double," and "Simple."[1]

---

1 Mother Mary St. Peter's explanation of Doubles, Semidoubles and Simples is highly simplified but is instructive nevertheless. Double-ranked feasts were themselves divided into a complicated hierarchy of classes (Doubles of I Class and II Class, Greater Doubles, etc.) which later came to be known simply as First Class, Second Class and Third Class feasts (the terms Double and Semidouble no longer being used); the Simple Feasts were termed as Commemorations.

There is a great deal more that you might learn, but for the present I will point out only one more item worth noticing about the most solemn of these feasts: these, you will find, are celebrated with an *Octave*. This means that the feast is of such high importance that its spirit is continued throughout eight days. During that time, the special Office and Mass of the feast are said on each of those eight days, provided that no other great feast comes in the way.

Chapter III

Something About the Liturgy of the Mass

OWEVER young you may be, you have learned, I am sure, that the holy sacrifice of the Mass is the first and greatest of all the acts of worship offered by the Church to Almighty God—and it can be offered to no other, not even to the Queen herself. It may be offered to Almighty God *in honor of* His Blessed Mother and the saints and angels—but *to* them, *never*.

Now, just as the holy sacrifice is the most important act of worship that can be offered to God by holy Church, so also the set forms of prayers that are used by the priest in the celebration of the Mass are the most important part of her Liturgy.

The celebration of the Mass may be divided into three parts:

1. From the very beginning, when the priest makes the sign of the cross, standing at the foot

of the altar, until the first ringing of the bell at the *Sanctus*;

2. From the *Sanctus* until the priest and the people have received holy communion;

3. From the prayer said by the priest after communion, until the very end of Mass.

In the first and last parts of the Mass, as in the Divine Office, certain prayers are changed according to the feast of the day on which the Mass is said. However, the second, most central part is so solemn that *the prayers are never changed*, no matter what feast may come—not even for Christmas or Easter.

How many of you own a Missal? Or, if happy enough to possess one, do you know how to use it? Some of you are too young for that, I dare say, so you will not remember the prayers said by the priest in their right order. Let us go through some of them.

When the priest (often called the *celebrant*, because he offers, or *celebrates*, holy Mass) comes to the foot of the altar, he makes the sign of the cross and says a Psalm[1] beginning: "Judge me, O God, and distinguish my cause from a nation that is not holy…" This is followed by the *Glory be*, certain Versicles and Responses, and then the *Confiteor*. The acolyte then repeats the *Confiteor*, the priest gives the Absolution, more Versicles and Responses are recited, and one or two short prayers are said. This done, we come to a bit of a Psalm called the *Introit*.

---

[1] Except in Masses for the dead, and from Passion Sunday till Holy Saturday.

The word *introit* means an entrance, or a beginning, and at this point the Mass may be said really to begin, for all that has come before is considered the Prayers at the Foot of the Altar, meant to prepare us for the Mass. The *Introit* is very important to us just now because it is the first prayer in the Mass that is changed for each feast—that is, it is *Proper* to the feast—for although the Psalm *Judica me* is sometimes left out, no other is said instead. If you find the *Introit* for the day in your Missal and read it carefully through, it will tell you what the character of the day is and something about it.

Perhaps an example will help to show what I mean.

The *Introit* for the third Mass on Christmas Day is: "A Child is born to us, and a Son is given to us; Whose government is upon His shoulder, and His Name shall be called The Angel of Great Counsel. Sing to the Lord a new Canticle, for He hath done wonderful things." No doubt you will agree this is a good choice to introduce the feast of the Nativity of Our Lord.

Immediately after the *Introit* the priest says the *Kyrie;* then the *Gloria*.[1] After this, he reads the next proper prayer in the Mass: this is the *Collect*—or *Collects*, for sometimes there is more than one—but the first always belongs especially to the feast, and, like the *Introit*, refers to it in some way. Here is the Collect for the Third Mass on Christmas Day: "Grant, we beseech Thee, almighty God, that the new birth of Thine only-

---
1 Except on penitential days and in Masses for the dead.

begotten Son in the flesh, may deliver us who are held by the old bondage under the yoke of sin."

The Latin word for a letter is *epistola*, and you have often heard letters called epistles, I dare say. No doubt you have also heard people speak of the Epistles of St. Paul and some of the other Apostles. Those Epistles were not mere letters such as you write to Mother or your sisters if you happen to be away from home. They were more like those papers called *Pastorals* which you have heard read sometimes after the Gospel on Sunday instead of a sermon, and which were written by your Bishop or Archbishop to all the Catholics of his diocese.

In these Epistles, the Apostles who wrote them explained many truths of faith to the early Christians, and taught them how to observe the Law of God. The Epistles are too long to be gone through all at once in every Mass, and so just a passage from one or other of them was—and still is—read each day in the Mass, and, like the *Introit* and *Collects*, this passage is changed according to the festival. Thus the Epistle is the third of our Propers.

Sometimes—more especially on the Queen's Festivals—a passage from some other part of the Bible is read instead of one from an Epistle, but it is never taken from the Gospels in the New Testament, nor from the Book of Psalms in the Old.

The *Gradual,* which comes after the Epistle, is generally a verse or two from some Psalm, and like the *Introit*, it usually expresses the character of the feast of the day—so, of course, it is also proper. The *Alleluia* is like it, though this part is replaced during Lent, and in Masses for the Dead, with a portion of a Psalm called the *Tract*.

The *Gospel* that is read in the Mass tells us the story of some part of Our Lord's Life—a miracle performed by Him, one of His parables, or a portion of His teaching—and it is connected with the feast. The *Gospel*, then, is the sixth of our Proper parts. The *Gospel* for Midnight Mass at Christmas is St. Luke's story of the birth of Our Lord in the stable at Bethlehem, while that for the Mass at daybreak on Christmas morning gives the story of the adoration of the shepherds.

On all Sundays and on great feasts the Nicene Creed is read. It is sometimes omitted during weekday Masses, but never exchanged for something else. The Creed marks the transition between the beginning part of the Mass, called the *Mass of the Catechumens*, which is meant to teach us and bring us closer to God, and the part we are entering now, called the *Mass of the Faithful*, in which our God comes to us in the Holy Sacrifice of the Altar.

The first part of the Mass of the Faithful is the *Offertory Antiphon*. This is a Psalm or prayer that used to be sung while the people made offerings, as in early days they did, at this part of the Mass. Like the other propers, it changes with the day and has reference to the feast.

The *Offertory Antiphon* proper to the feast of the Assumption is: "Mary is assumed into heaven; the angels rejoice, praising they bless the Lord."

Having said several offertory prayers, during which he prepares the bread and wine which are to become our Lord's body and blood, the priest will then wash his hands while reciting part of a Psalm that begins with the word *Lavabo*, meaning "I will wash." This done, he turns to us and in a very special way invites us to join our own sacrifices and prayers with his at the altar.

He is about to enter that special part of the Mass that I told you about—the part that is unchangeable—but before he does, he will turn once more to the altar and silently speak a prayer called the *Secret*. Now, this is not really a secret like the kind you share with a friend; it merely means that it is spoken silently, while those spoken before and after it are spoken aloud. The *Secret* is the eighth of our proper prayers and, like the *Collects*, it presents to God our special petitions for this feast. The *Secret* for the Third Mass for Christmas is: "Sanctify our oblations, O Lord, by the new birth of Thy only-begotten Son, and cleanse us from the stains of our sins."

Now we arrive at the *Preface*, which introduces the *Canon* (that is, the most solemn part of the Mass) and which sometimes changes for the feast. The prayers used during the *Canon* itself never change, but after the solemn Sacrifice is completed and the priest and people have received Holy Communion, the prayers which follow, called the *Communion* and *Post-Communion*, are the last of our propers belonging to the feast.

Have you found this chapter long, and rather dry?

Well, we devote a great deal of time and pains to the study of some matters—to working examples, for instance, to the Amendments of the Constitution, and to the Geography of the United States. They are all very good and it is right to try to learn as much as we can about them. But for Catholic children—and men and women, too—it is a thousand times more right that we should learn how to honor our Queen.

Part II

The Queen's Anniversaries

Apparuit Dominus in flamma ignis de medio rubi. Exod. 3.

Regressus invenit germinasse virgam Aaron. Num. 17.

Chapter IV

The Immaculate Conception

December 8

"I will greatly rejoice in the Lord, and my soul shall be joyful in my God; for He hath clothed me with the garments of salvation, and with the robe of justice hath He covered me, as a bride adorned with her jewels. I will exalt Thee, O God, for Thou hast upheld me, and hast not made my enemies to rejoice over me." —Introit for Mass of the Feast.

HE Immaculate Conception! I hear one of you saying, "That feast comes at the very end of the year; what a funny time to begin at!"
You think so? Then please read very attentively and you will find that, while you are quite right after your own fashion, you are somewhat mistaken, too.

The feast of the Immaculate Conception of the Queen is kept on the 8th of December, and December is the last month of the year according to the arrangement of the calendar that you know something about. But December is the *first* part of the year according to another arrangement of the calendar of which you know probably very little, perhaps nothing at all.

Did you ever hear of Advent?

"Oh, yes; it comes before Christmas, and the Fridays are fast-days; the grownups don't have any breakfast."

"Oh, yes, I like Advent. They sing the *Alma Redemptoris Mater* in our church after Vespers on Sundays, and—"

Yes; and—?

"Well, I was going to say, we buy our presents in Advent. We have to, or they wouldn't be ready for Christmas."

You are both right; but I can tell you something else about Advent. In the Church it is counted as the first part of the year—of the *ecclesiastical* year, or year of the Church. If you look in your Missal (or in that of somebody else if you do not own a Missal as yet) you will find the Masses of the saints whose feasts occur in Advent put first of all. The very first will be the Mass of St. Andrew, whose feast falls on the 29th of November.

The Immaculate Conception, which we celebrate on the 8th of December, is the first of the Queen's Festivals that occurs in the ecclesiastical year, so for that reason alone, this is the right place for it. Then also, the mystery of the Immaculate Conception is the first of Our Lady's life, and it is well to begin at the beginning.

Lastly, many persons have believed that of all the wonderful privileges bestowed upon our Lady, the privilege of her Immaculate Conception is that which she loves the best, because it is the privilege which renders her most pleasing in the sight of God.

And what is this great privilege? What is the meaning of the Immaculate Conception?

It means that from the very first moment of her existence, our blessed Mother, Mary the Queen, never had upon her pure soul the slightest spot of sin. The devil never, for one single instant, had her in his power; and her soul was so pure and stainless that not even Baptism—had it been instituted—could have made it whiter or more pure.

You know, for you have learned it in your Catechism, that your soul and mine—everybody's in fact—was once stained with that sin called Original, which we inherited from Adam through his eating the forbidden fruit. But Mary, by the power of God, through the future merits of her Son, escaped that inheritance and was never stained with Original Sin, because it was not fitting that the future Mother of God should be for a single moment under the power of the devil, His great enemy. This is what we mean by the Immaculate Conception. Mary was conceived without Original Sin.

The greater number of Catholics, especially those who were very devout to the Blessed Mother, have always believed in this mystery, and, of course, it has always been true. For many hundreds of years people took it for granted, although it is true that some learned, and indeed saintly men had disputes about it now and then. But in 1854, Pope Pius IX settled the matter once for all by declaring the Immaculate Conception of the Blessed Virgin Mary to be an Article of Faith, in a special Apostolic letter, called a *Bull* or *Bulla*, after the leaden stamp with which it is sealed and made official.

The feast of the Immaculate Conception has been kept in the Church from very early times. It was first observed in the East—that is, in all the Christian countries situated to the east of Italy: Turkey, Greece, all the west of Asia, Egypt, and the north of Africa.

In Western Europe, the feast was first observed in Spain in the ninth century. A little later it was established in England, and, shortly after that, was kept throughout the Church.

In the year 1760 a king of Spain, Charles III, obtained permission from Pope Clement XIII to choose Our Lady of the Immaculate Conception as the Titular Patroness of Spain; and our own country, America, enjoys the same privilege. For this reason the feast is kept here as a Holy Day of Obligation; and we are obliged to hear holy Mass and do no more servile work than is absolutely necessary on that day.

The feast of the Immaculate Conception is ranked as a *Double* of the First Class.[1] It is one of those very important feasts that has an *Octave*—that is, the Mass and other offices of the feast are said or sung during the next eight days—and all those eight days are *Semi-doubles*. During the octave, the priest wears white vestments at holy Mass, and the *Credo* (Nicene Creed) is always said after the Gospel.

---
1 See page 11 for an explanation of this ranking.

Now it is time for a story.

I told you that even learned and holy men have sometimes doubted the truth of the mystery of the Immaculate Conception; and there had been many disputes about it before Pope Pius IX declared it to be an Article of Faith. It happened as far back as the thirteenth century that one of these disputes was going on, and a holy Franciscan Friar was much grieved, because he loved Our Lady dearly and valued her honor above all things. So he determined to take part in the dispute, and to do his best to prove that the Mother of God never had been for one single moment under the power of Satan.

The debate was to be held in a public church, very many people were to be present, and Duns Scotus (that was the name of the Friar) knew that much depended upon the words which he should speak that day. He knew also that those Doctors who did not agree with him were very learned—some of them were very saintly too—and they had strong reasons for their side of the question. (It would be useless to tell you what these reasons were, for until you are older you could not possibly understand them, and of course since the Pope has settled the matter they are not reasons at all any more.) But Duns Scotus knew that they were looked upon as powerful then, and that if he were to depend upon his own knowledge and cleverness only, he might fail to make people see the truth about the Queen; so he resolved to get her to help him.

As he passed before a statue of Mary that stood by the wayside—you may still see such in some of the Catholic countries of Europe—he knelt before it and said: *Dignare me laudare te, Virgo sacrata: Da mihi virtutem contra hostes tuos.* The English of his prayer is: "Make me worthy to praise thee, O Sacred Virgin: Give me strength against thy enemies."

And the gracious Lady, who wished to encourage her faithful servant, caused the statue to bow its head as if to assure him that she would indeed give him all the strength he needed, and would teach him what he must say.

Duns Scotus rose from his knees and went to the Church, where he spoke with such wisdom and power that he convinced all those who had opposed him. He gave such clear reasons why the Mother of God should have been conceived without sin, that the truth of the mystery has seldom been called in question by anyone of importance since. The prayer "*Dignare me laudare te*," is now part of the Liturgy of the Church, and you may hear it chanted after Our Lady's antiphon, the *Salve Regina*, at the end of Vespers on any Sunday between the feast of the Purification and Palm Sunday.

The miraculous statue of the Queen is no longer to be seen. The disputation took place in Paris, and although the statue was shown for many ages afterward, it seems to have been destroyed during the terrible French Revolution which put an end to so much that was precious and beautiful in France.

Some people will tell you that this story is only a legend, and that Our Lady never bowed her head to Duns Scotus at all. Well, you are not bound to believe it; it is not an Article of Faith, but we are very sure and certain that it was not impossible. The Queen could have done much more even than that, had she so chosen.

Sapientia ædificavit sibi do- mum, excidit ... Prov. 9, 1.

Rursum dimisit columbam ex arca. At illa .. Gen. 8, 10.

Chapter V

The Nativity of the Blessed Virgin

September 8

> "Hail, holy Parent, who didst bring forth the King Who rules Heaven and earth forever. My heart hath uttered a good word; I speak my works to the King."
>
> —Introit of Mass for Feast.

I THINK you will find it less difficult to learn something of the feasts of Our Lady if we take them in the natural order, going through those which commemorate events in her life first. Afterward we will speak of those which have been instituted by the Church in honor of the Queen for other reasons.

Did you ever notice, or has any one told you, that the Church seldom keeps the natural birthday of a saint? Indeed, I know of only three which she honors in that way. The feasts days we celebrate generally are kept to commemorate the day of the saint's death, as this might well be considered their "birthday in heaven." The day of a saint's death is especially revered if that saint was a martyr, as St. Agnes and St. Sebastian, whose feasts are celebrated on the 21st and 22nd of January; or the translation or removal of his or her relics from one place to another, as the feast of St. Swithin, July the 15th; or the dedication of some great church under his or her invocation, as the Dedication of the Church of SS. Peter and Paul, November the 18th.

The reason why natural birthdays are not celebrated by the Church is that in consequence of Adam's sin, we come into the world with a stain upon our souls, which is certainly not a thing to rejoice over. We keep our birthdays at home because we are glad to be alive, and grateful to God for having created us. This is quite right—in its way—but Mother Church looks higher, and rejoices over the eternal good of her children, which is only really attained when they have passed through "the Valley of the Shadow of Death" and have "entered into the joy of their Lord."

Still, there are three natural birthdays kept by the Church, and you may find them marked as feasts in the Missal and in all Catholic calendars. The first of these is the Nativity of Our Lord, which is kept on Christmas Day, December 25th.

"Of course; but Our Lord was not born in Original Sin. He came to help us get clear of it."

Exactly. There are more reasons for keeping that birthday than we could tell in a day. The next of these three natural birthdays is the 24th of June, when the Church celebrates the Nativity of St. John the Baptist.

"Yes; but he was cleansed from Original Sin before he was born; when Our Lady visited St. Elizabeth."

So he was, and since no stain of sin ever came near the pure soul of Mary the Queen, the Church keeps her birthday too. It falls on the 8th of September and is a Double with an Octave.

And what is the story of the Nativity of the Queen?

The Gospels do not give it. From not one of the four do we learn anything about Our Lady's life before the Annunciation, excepting that she was espoused to St. Joseph, that she lived at Nazareth, and that she was descended from David.

But a tradition has been handed down to us from very early ages which has always been piously believed, although it is not an Article of Faith.

Some fourteen or fifteen years before the birth of Our Lord, there lived in Palestine a very holy man named Joachim, who belonged to the tribe of Juda and to the family of David, so that he was of royal race. He was married to a woman called Anne (or Anna) who was holy like himself and noble, too. It seems likely that she belonged to the family of Aaron, from which the Jewish priests were chosen, and if so, she was of the tribe of Levi. They were good and prosperous as far as the goods of the world are concerned, yet they were not quite happy, because Almighty God had not seen fit to bless them with children. So they were afraid that perhaps He was displeased with them, although they tried to serve Him as well as they could.

But one day when Joachim and Anne had both grown old waiting and praying and practising resignation to the will of God, an angel appeared to Joachim and told him to take comfort, for he and Anne would have a daughter who should be a joy and blessing to the whole world. Not long after this, the little Mary was born, and surely there has been on earth only One whose birth has been a greater blessing than hers. Her birthday is kept, as you know, on the 8th of September. Father Faber says in his beautiful hymn to St. Anne:—

>Oh blest be the day when old earth bore its fruit,
>   The fairest of daughters it ever had seen,
>In the village that lies at the white mountain foot,
>   And the angels sang songs to the young Nazarene!

I ought to tell you, though, that it is generally believed that the Queen was born, not in Nazareth, as this hymn suggests, but in Jerusalem, where her parents owned a house.

Chapter VI

Feast of the Holy Name of Mary

Sunday within the Octave of the Nativity of Mary

"All the rich among the people shall entreat thy countenance. After her shall virgins be brought to the King: her neighbors shall be brought to thee in gladness and rejoicing. My heart hath uttered a good word; I speak my works to the King."
—Introit of the Feast.

OF course, as she was entirely free from sin, the future Mother of God needed no Baptism; in any case she could not have been baptized, because the sacraments had not yet been instituted; but, like all other children, she needed a name. It was the custom among the Jews, who were her people, to name the little ones when they were eight days old, and they were very particular as to the name which they chose.

That given to the Queen was Mary, which in one language means "Star of the Sea," and in another, "Lady" or "Sovereign." The actual Hebrew name, however, is not really Mary, but *Miriam*, which you may notice was the name of that sister of Moses who was set by her mother to watch the ark made of rushes wherein the future savior of his people was set afloat upon the waters of the Nile.

We are told of the Most Holy Name of Jesus that, *"At the name of Jesus every knee shall bow, of them that are in heaven, of them that are on earth, and of them that are under the earth,"* and that *"There is no other name under heaven whereby we may be saved."*

And so, too, there is great power in the name of Mary. When a little child is afraid of anything, its first thought is to call upon its mother, and a strange mother she would be who did not answer the call if she could. Our Mother in heaven can always answer our call—and she always will.

There is a pretty story told of a parrot which had learned to say the two words "Hail, Mary." It happened one day that this parrot escaped from its cage and flew into the open air, where it was seen and pursued by a hawk. The poor terrified bird screamed out "Hail, Mary! Hail, Mary! Hail, Mary!" and behold! the savage hawk flew round and round as if it were dizzy, and then fell dead to the ground. The Queen would not turn a deaf ear even to a parrot that invoked her.

It is a fact that a little boy of seven years old once tumbled into a rapid stream and was carried away by the current. He was much too frightened to remember his prayers, but he did remember his Mother. Like the parrot he shouted "Hail, Mary! Hail, Mary!" with all his might, and at once found himself swimming against the stream although he had never swum before in his short life.

The poet William Wordsworth once wrote, "Nature never did betray the heart that loved her;" and I dare say he was right. But, children, it is a thousand times more true to say that Mary never did refuse to grant the prayer of any one who invoked her name. So when you are in trouble, when you need something, even when you only *wish* for something, follow the counsel of St. Bernard: *Call on Mary.*

Of course you all know the *Memorare*. If there should be any one amongst you who does not, that child had better learn it at once:

> Remember, O most gracious Virgin Mary,
> that never was it known
> that anyone who fled to thy protection,
> implored thy help,
> or sought thine intercession
> was left unaided.

> Inspired by this confidence,
> I fly unto thee, O Virgin of virgins, my mother;
> to thee do I come, before thee I stand,
> sinful and sorrowful.
> O Mother of the Word Incarnate,
> despise not my petitions,
> but in thy mercy hear and answer me. Amen.

The festival of the Holy Name of Mary is a Double and has a Mass of its own. Because it commemorates the eighth day after the Nativity of Mary, the feast of her Holy Name was was always celebrated on the Octave day of her Nativity when it was first kept in Spain in 1513. Later, when it came to be observed throughout the Church beginning in 1683, it was decided to give this special feast the honor of occupying the Sunday within that Octave.

Chapter VII

The Presentation of the Blessed Virgin Mary

November 21

"O God, by Whose Will the Blessed Mary ever Virgin, being herself the dwelling-place of the Holy Spirit, was this day presented in the Temple, grant, we beseech Thee, that through her intercession we may be found worthy to be presented in the Temple of Thy Glory." —Collect for Feast.

BY a law of God, given especially to the Jewish people, they were obliged to offer to Him the eldest or "first-born" son of every family, that this child might be consecrated to His service. If the parents did not wish to leave the little one in the Temple to be brought up there, they *redeemed* him, or bought him back at the cost of a lamb if they were rich people, or of two doves if they were poor. The Prophet Samuel was left with the High-Priest by his parents; but Our Lord was offered in fulfillment of the law, and then redeemed by St. Joseph for two doves or pigeons, because it was the

will of His heavenly Father that the holy Child should remain under the care of His Blessed Mother.

Strictly speaking, this law did not apply to little girls, but out of devotion many persons took their baby daughters to the Temple and consecrated them to the service of God. They did not remain there always, but were taken back at the age of thirteen or fourteen and married to someone chosen by their parents or guardians. Nobody thought of becoming a Religious in those days, because Our Lord had not yet said, "If thou wilt be perfect, go, sell what thou hast, and give to the poor and come, follow Me."

A very ancient tradition tells us that when the little Queen was given to Joachim and Anne in their old age, they determined out of gratitude to devote her to the special service of God. So at three years old she was taken to the Temple and given into the charge of the priests to be brought up. It is piously believed that Mary was already gifted with the use of reason, and that she knew and understood what was being done. She climbed up the fifteen steps that led to the Temple without help from anybody, so eager was the future Mother of God to give herself entirely to His service.

The feast of the Presentation of the Blessed Virgin Mary in the Temple was kept in the East in very early times, but it was not observed in the West until 1372, at a city in the south of France called Avignon. In the sixteenth century, Pope Sixtus V ordered that the Office of the feast should be recited throughout the Church.

The Presentation of the Blessed Virgin Mary

The Presentation is one of the many festivals of the Queen which belong in a very especial manner to *children*, and to *school-children*, for the day on which she entered the Temple was the first of her life at school. She began to learn then all the things that Jewish girls and women were expected to know when they undertook the care of homes of their own.

So in all your difficulties and troubles—even when the lessons are difficult or the "Examples" *will not* come right, just tell her about it. The little Queen had troubles in school, too, and has not forgotten them. She will help you out of yours when no one else can, except of course her divine Son—and He likes His Mother to ask Him.

Chapter VIII

The Espousals of the Blessed Virgin Mary

January 23

"Thou art happy, O holy Virgin Mary, and most worthy of all praise; because from thee arose the Sun of Justice, Christ the Lord." —Gradual of Mass for Feast.

HILE the little Queen was living in the Temple and learning to spin, to weave, to sew, to take care of a house, and to sing the praises of God, nobody guessed that she was anything more than the other children of the Temple who worked and studied and sang. Perhaps it was remarked that she kept silence better, that she wrought more diligently, and had a greater love of prayer than her companions. Those who had charge of her were aware that she belonged to a noble family, and was descended from David the Prophet King. That was all.

But God knew that she was to be the Mother of His Son, and that it would be necessary to find some wise and saintly person who would take care of and protect her and the holy Child. It is generally believed that Joachim and Anne were dead before the Blessed Virgin was quite twelve years old; so she remained under the care of the priests in the Temple until she had reached the age of thirteen or fourteen. Then it became the duty of her guardians to choose a spouse for their ward from among the unmarried men of her own family, since that was the custom among the Jews.

The little Queen would have preferred to remain in the Temple. It is believed by many wise and holy persons that she had even made a vow to consecrate her whole life to God. But this was a very unusual thing to do at that time, and the priests did not understand or approve of it. Mary knew that her duty was to obey, and she consented to accept the husband proposed for her.

A pretty legend has come down to us from the early ages of the Church which says that the priests were puzzled as to whom they should choose to be the spouse of the Queen out of the number of young men of the tribe of Juda who were anxious to be accepted. Then the High-Priest was inspired to tell them all to bring their staves to him, and he placed these staves in a certain part of the Temple and left them there all night. He prayed that Almighty God would vouchsafe, by means of these staves, to make known his holy will; and when they were brought out in the morning that which bore the name of Joseph was found to be covered with beautiful flowers, and the Priest knew that the Queen was to be given into the care of the owner of that rod.

Among the Jews, marriage was probably not a religious ceremony as it is among Christians. It had not been raised to the dignity of a sacrament then, and was only a contract or agreement between two persons. But a wedding was a grand event all the same, and it was celebrated with festivities that lasted several days. We may learn something of the ceremonies from the parables of Our Lord, for many of these refer to weddings.

We know from the Parable of the Ten Virgins that the bridegroom and the bride were accompanied to their home (where the festival was held) by a grand procession with lamps or torches. In another parable, we are told that the number of guests invited was very great, so that "beeves and fatlings" (or as we should say, oxen and calves) were killed and dressed for their entertainment. And wine was provided for the guests, for at the Marriage Feast at Cana in Galilee there was not enough, and Our Lord, who was present, worked His first miracle at the request of His Blessed Mother, by turning water into wine.

Neither St. Joseph nor Our Lady was very rich, so their festival could not be very splendid, but we may be sure that they observed the customs of their people so far as they could.

When it was all over, they journeyed to Nazareth—seventy miles from the Temple and Jerusalem—and St. Joseph took care of the Queen, and later of her divine Son, for the next thirty years.

The feast of the Espousals is a Double.

Chapter IX

The Annunciation of the Blessed Virgin Mary

March 25

"Hail, Mary, full of grace, the Lord is with thee. Blessed art thou among women, and blessed is the Fruit of thy womb."
—Offertory of the Mass for the Feast.

THIS is the first event in the life of the Queen about which we are clearly told in the Gospel itself. All the rest so far has come down to us by *tradition*. That is, we learn it from the writings of holy men who lived in the early ages of the Church, and these learned it from others who lived in ages earlier still, and who probably learned the stories in the very beginning from Our Lord's Apostles, or even from Our Lady herself.

In the first chapter of his gospel St. Luke tells us:

> At that time the Angel Gabriel was sent from God into a city of Galilee called Nazareth, to a Virgin espoused to a man whose name was Joseph of the House of David; and the Virgin's name was Mary.

> And the Angel being come in said unto her: Hail, full of grace, the Lord is with thee; blessed art thou amongst women.[1]

When Gabriel said this, the Queen was troubled at hearing such high praise from a stranger and, "Thought within herself what manner of salutation this should be."[2] But the Angel told her not to be afraid, for she had found favor with God. He then told her that she would have a Son whose name was to be called Jesus.

> He shall be called great, and shall be the Son of the Most High, and the Lord God shall give unto Him the throne of David His father, and He shall reign in the House of David forever. And of His kingdom there shall be no end.[3]

Then the Queen said: "Behold the handmaid of the Lord. Be it done unto me according to thy word,"[4] and in that moment, "The Word was made Flesh, and dwelt among us."[5]

The Blessed Mother had a cousin, Elizabeth, who was very much older than herself and lived a long way from Nazareth among the mountains, in "the hill country of Judea." Elizabeth's husband Zachary was a priest of the Temple in Jerusalem, and for many years he and his wife had wished for nothing on earth so much as to have a son, but they were still childless.

The archangel told the Queen that Almighty God had at last granted the prayers of His servants, and that in three months from that time, Elizabeth would

---

1 Luke 1:26-28.   2 *Ibid.*, 29.   3 *Ibid.*, 31-32.
4 *Ibid.*, 38.   5 John 1:14.

be made happy by the birth of a son. At this news, the Gospel goes on to say that Mary rose up with haste, and went down from Nazareth to visit her cousin.

The feast of the Annunciation is a Double, and has a Mass of its own. It was formerly a Holy Day of Obligation—that is, the faithful were obliged to observe the day as if it were a Sunday, by hearing holy Mass and doing no unnecessary servile work. All true servants of the Queen, and loving Children of Mary, go to Mass on the Annunciation, although not actually commanded to do so under pain of sin.

The Church has kept this day as a festival from the very earliest times. Indeed, it is believed by some writers to have been instituted by the Apostles.

As the 25th of March almost always falls in Passion or Holy Week—the most sorrowful times of the year—it was decided long ago, at the beginning of the seventh century, that the Annunciation should not be kept on that day any more, but on the 18th of December. However, it was soon restored to its own proper day, on condition that if it should fall on Easter Sunday or on any of the three last days of Holy Week, its celebration shall be transferred to some day after Easter.

The *Angelus* which we say three times every day is a devotion in honor of the mystery of the Annunciation, and one which Mary loves very dearly, so we must try to say it as devoutly as we can. Father Faber declares that but too many people say it as if they "were praying against a bell"[1] to try who can finish first. Perhaps if we remember that the reverence with which we say the *Angelus* will help to make up to the Queen and her divine Son for all the bad and profane words with which they are often insulted, we shall be less likely to "gabble."

For those of you who have not yet learned to pray the *Angelus*, it is not too soon to begin:

> V. The Angel of the Lord declared to Mary:
> R. And she conceived of the Holy Spirit.
>
> Hail Mary...
>
> V. Behold the handmaid of the Lord:
> R. Be it done unto me according to Thy word.
>
> Hail Mary...
>
> V. And the Word was made Flesh:
> R. And dwelt among us.
>
> Hail Mary...
>
> V. Pray for us, O Holy Mother of God:
> R. That we may be made worthy of the promises of Christ.
>
> LET US PRAY:
> Pour forth, we beseech Thee, O Lord, Thy grace into our hearts; that we, to whom the incarnation of Christ, Thy Son, was made known by the message of an angel, may by His Passion and Cross be brought to the glory of His Resurrection, through the same Christ Our Lord. Amen.

A holy priest who was giving a retreat to a number of convent girls, and who has since gone to his reward, R.I.P., told them that he once had the happiness of

---

1 *Spiritual Conferences*, 1859.

seeing and conversing with Bernadette, the peasant girl who saw and spoke with the Blessed Mother at Lourdes. This priest asked Bernadette to tell him something in connection with her visions which she had not mentioned to any one else, and after considering for a few moments she said: "Once while I was speaking to the Queen of Heaven, she looked away from me and seemed to pay no attention to what I said. I was grieved then, and feared that in some way I must have offended the Blessed Mother, and I said: 'O, holy Virgin, why do you turn your face from me? Have I been so unhappy as to offend you?' But she said, 'No, my child, you have not offended me; but at this moment the *Angelus* bells are ringing from the churches, and I am listening to the *Ave Marias* of my faithful people, for they can utter no words in my hearing that I love as well.'"

By the way, children, you very often see the letters "R.I.P." Do you know what they mean when written after the name of some one who is dead?

They stand for the Latin words *Requiescat in pace,* "May he (or she) rest in peace."

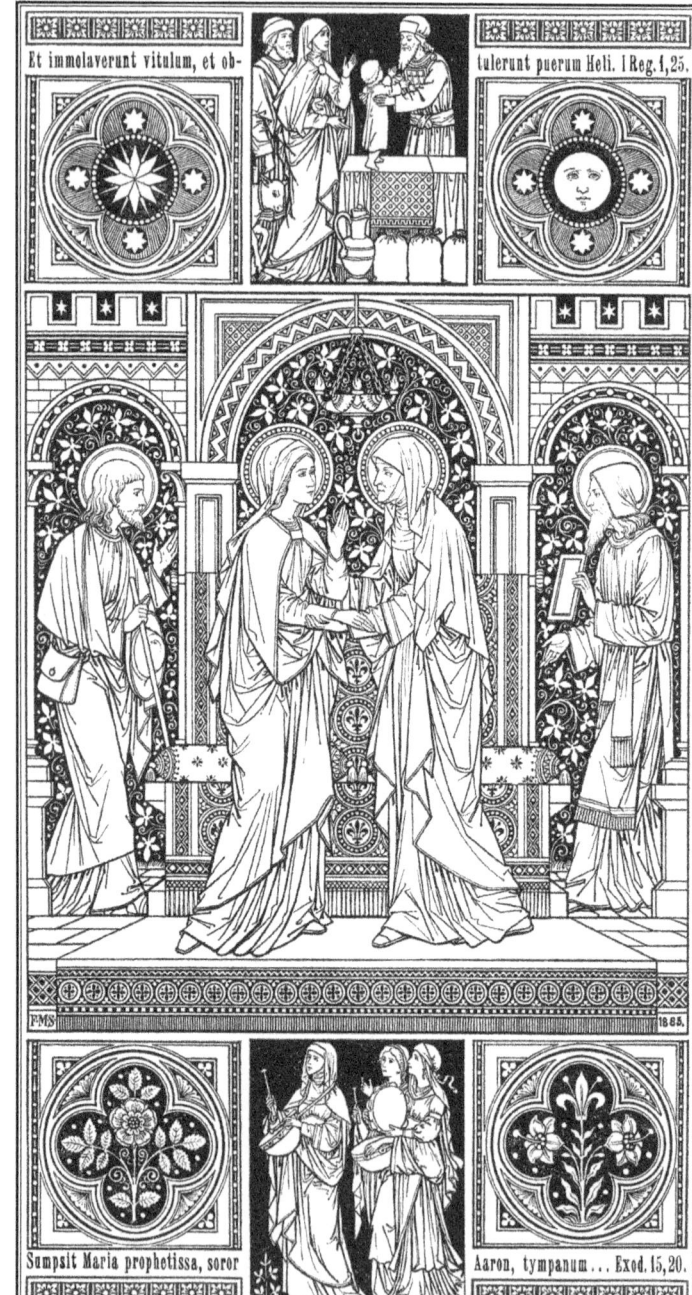

Et immolaverunt vitulum, et obtulerunt puerum Heli. I Reg. 1, 25.

Sumpsit Maria prophetissa, soror Aaron, tympanum... Exod. 15, 20.

Chapter X

The Visitation of the Blessed Virgin Mary

July 2

> *"Thou art blessed, O Virgin Mary, who didst bear the Creator of all things. Thou didst bring forth Him Who made thee, and thou remainest forever a Virgin."*
> —Offertory of the Feast.

At that time, Mary rising up, went with haste into the hill country, unto a city of Juda. And she entered into the house of Zachary and saluted Elizabeth.[1]

he Queen had traveled nearly seventy miles; it is most likely that she had walked the whole distance from Nazareth to the place where Elizabeth lived, in Ain-Karim, in order to give her cousin a pleasure and to tell her how glad she was that a little son was to be born to her cousin and Zachary at last.

Almighty God had revealed to Elizabeth, who was a very holy person indeed, that Mary was to bring His only-begotten Son into the world, and

> Elizabeth was filled with the Holy Ghost, and she cried with a loud voice saying: Blessed art thou

---

1   Luke 1:39-40.

among women, and blessed is the Fruit of thy womb. And whence is this to me that the Mother of my Lord should come to me?[1]

You have heard, I suppose, that when kings or queens pay visits they often make presents to those who receive them as guests. The King and Queen of heaven were not likely to be less generous than earthly sovereigns, and at that moment a grace was bestowed upon the unborn child of Elizabeth—his soul was cleansed from Original Sin.

Then the Queen answered the salutation of her cousin by saying her own beautiful canticle, the *Magnificat*:

> And Mary said: My soul doth magnify the Lord, and my spirit hath rejoiced in God my Saviour. Because he hath regarded the humility of his handmaid; for behold from henceforth all generations shall call me blessed. Because he that is mighty, hath done great things to me; and holy is his name. And his mercy is from generation unto generations, to them that fear him. He hath shewed might in his arm: he hath scattered the proud in the conceit of their heart. He hath put down the mighty from their seat, and hath exalted the humble. He hath filled the hungry with good things; and the rich he hath sent empty away. He hath received Israel his servant, being mindful of his mercy: As he spoke to our fathers, to Abraham and to his seed for ever.[2]

You should learn Our Lady's own canticle by heart—it is not so very long, and not more difficult than "Hail Columbia," or "My Country, 'tis of thee."

---

1 Luke 1:41-43.   2 *Ibid.*, 46-55.

Say it when you feel very happy, because "He that is mighty" has done some great thing for you.

The festival of the Visitation is a Double. All the antiphons at Vespers are composed of sentences taken from the Gospel of the feast—the first being:

> Mary rising up, went with haste into the hill country, unto a city of Juda.[1]

There is a very pretty legend told about the *Magnificat*. You know that at Vespers five Psalms are sung or chanted, and that these are changed according to the season in which they are recited. Thus, the second Psalm in the Sunday Vespers is that which begins *Confitebor tibi Domini*; the second Psalm in the Vespers of the Visitation begins *Laudate Pueri*, and so on; but in all Vespers, after the last Psalm, the *Magnificat* is recited. Our Lady's canticle is never changed for another—never left out.

Now, it happened once upon a time that there stood, in the midst of a forest, a convent wherein dwelt certain monks who loved the Queen before all things, saving only her divine Son; and being gifted by God with voices above the common, they honored her with sweet music and chanting every day.

But as time went on the monks grew old and their voices became cracked and tuneless. They made music no more and no novices came to fill their places and sing as *they* had been used to do. Still, they did their best for love of God and Our Lady, and chanted with

---
1 Luke 1:39.

such right good will and such hideous clamor that the very birds in the trees round the monastery took fright and flew away. Then the Abbot said: "My brethren, we can no longer make music by singing. In future we will read the Psalms. Only the *Magnificat* will we chant in Mary's honor as best we can."

So the brethren read the Office after that, chanting only the *Magnificat*. That they would have read as they read the others, for they were greatly ashamed of the discord they made among them and to see the birds take flight every day. But they obeyed their Abbot and sang on; and this went on for several years. Then came at last a novice to the convent, and his voice was as the voice of an angel, whereat all greatly rejoiced, and they bade him sing Our Lady's *Magnificat* every day. And ever as he sang there was a smile upon his lips and vanity in his heart, as he thought upon the poor old brethren whose singing was such that the birds fled in terror from the sound. And the monks thanked God daily that at last there was one among them who could worthily sing the Canticle of the Queen.

But one evening as they sat in choir an angel stood in their midst. His face was grave and sad, and his voice, as he spoke to the Lord Abbot, though wondrous sweet, was almost stern.

"I am sent hither by my Lord and King," he said, "to ask wherefore the strains of the Queen's *Magnificat* no longer arise at eventide from your choir? For many a long year hath it made melody in the courts of heaven.

He would know wherefore ye are silent now, and wherefore for these many eventides its music hath not reached the ear of God."

The angel waited for no answer, but straightway vanished from their sight, while the young singer bowed his head in shame upon his breast at thought of his vanity—and with one accord the ancient brethren raised discordant voices and sang the Canticle of the Queen.

On that eventide there was once more melody in heaven although in the forest the birds were terrified and flew away.

You are all quick enough to catch the lesson taught by that story, I think.

The mystery of the Visitation has always been honored in the Church, but the day has been kept as a feast only since 1263, when St. Bonaventure was General of the Franciscan Order. He commanded that it should be observed in all his convents, and very soon its observance spread throughout the Church.

It is said, too, that St. Bonaventure was the first to arrange the *Angelus* prayers as we say them now, though it was nearly two hundred years before his time that Pope Urban had ordered the "Ave Maria Bell" to be rung at sunrise, noontide, and sunset.

Chapter XI

The Expectation of the Blessed Virgin Mary

December 18

"Behold, a Virgin shall conceive and bring forth a Son, Alleluia."
—Part of Gradual of Mass for the Feast.

OU learned in Chapter IX that because the Annunciation is one of the most joyful of all the Queen's Festivals, and yet it falls nearly always either in Passion or Holy Week—the saddest and most penitential times of the whole year—the celebration of the feast of the Annunciation was transferred in the seventh century from the 25th of March to December the 18th. But in spite of sadness and penitence, the faithful could not help rejoicing with their Mother on what they believed to be her own day, so very soon the Annunciation was put back again.

In the meantime people had grown accustomed to honoring the Queen on the 18th of December, and were unwilling to give up the feast altogether. Thus it was decided that on this day, which is just eight days before Christmas, a festival should be kept in honor of the Blessed Mother's expectation of the speedy coming of her divine Son.

How happy she must have been at the thought that in one little week she would see Him! She had gone back to Nazareth after visiting her cousin, and knew that all that long journey into Judea must be taken again, for the prophets had declared that the Messias would be born in Bethlehem—and it was the middle of winter.

But the Queen did not mind all that. He must come into the world where and when He would, and whatever He willed was right. But to see Him in a week! To hold Him in her arms, a tiny Baby! To have Him for her very own! I suppose children who are preparing for their first communion can understand better than many others what Our Lady felt then.

Do you know Father Faber's beautiful hymn "Like the Dawning of the Morning"? It is the hymn for the feast of the Expectation, and I am sorry that we have not space for the whole of it here. But you must have a few verses, and look up the others in your hymn book.

> Like the Dawning of the Morning
>   On the Mountain's golden heights,
> Like the breaking of the moonbeams
>   On the gloom of cloudy nights,
> Like a secret told by Angels
>   Getting known upon the earth
> Is the Mother's Expectation
>   Of Messias' speedy birth!

> Thou wert happy, blessed Mother!
>   With the very bliss of heaven,
> Since the angel's salutation
>   In thy raptured ear was given;
> Since the Ave of that midnight,
>   When thou wert anointed Queen,
> Like a river overflowing
>   Hath the grace within thee been.
>
> And the sweet strains of the psalmist
>   Were a joy beyond control,
> And the visions of the prophets
>   Burnt like transports in thy soul;
> But the Burden that was growing,
>   And was felt so tenderly—
> It was heaven—it was heaven—
>   Come before its time to thee!
>
> Thou hast waited, Child of David,
>   And thy waiting now is o'er!
> Thou hast seen Him, Blessed Mother,
>   And wilt see Him evermore!
> Oh, His human Face and Features,
>   They were passing sweet to see!
> Thou beholdest them this moment;
>   Mother, show them now to me![1]

The feast of the Expectation of Our Lady is a greater Double, and the Vespers are the same as on the Annunciation. The Mass said is the Mass of Our Lady in Advent, with the exception of that portion of the Gradual which you may find written at the head of this chapter.

---

1 "Like the Dawning of the Morning," is actually the first stanza of "Our Lady's Expectation," Fr Frederick W. Faber, *Hymns*, 1861.

Chapter XII

The Purification of the Blessed Virgin Mary

February 2

"Simeon received an answer from the Holy Ghost, that he should not see death, until he had seen the Christ of the Lord."
—Communion of Mass of the Feast.

AS YOU know, some of the grandest festivals of the year come after the feast of the Expectation, but while Our Lady has a great share in all of them, they are not so entirely hers as to be—strictly speaking—festivals of the Queen.

Christmas Day is the birthday of the King. He has three Masses, and the First and Second Vespers are all His. The Circumcision is His Name Day, and the Epiphany is the celebration of His Manifestation to the Gentiles.

The Purification, on the 2nd of February, is the first festival after that of the Expectation which is wholly and entirely the Queen's. Of course, we must remember always that the lives of the Blessed Mother and her divine Son are so closely bound up with each other that both must have a share in every festival that is kept in honor of either. I am sure you all understand that.

Now I must tell you that the Jews were people who had very many customs which were unlike those of other nations, and which marked them out as a people apart. Some of these customs were observed in their own homes, and in daily life; others had to do with religion and the worship of God. Among the latter was one to whose observance they were bound by a law, commanding every Jewish woman to go up to the Temple on the fortieth day after the birth of a son, and there offer the child to the Lord, with a sacrifice—a pair of doves or two young pigeons. In the Temple the Priest prayed over the mother and her son, and presented the little one to God if he were the firstborn of his parents. But he might be redeemed, if they chose, by the sacrifice of a lamb or another dove. We are told that St. Joseph and the Queen carried the little King to the Temple when He was forty days old "and did for Him according to the Law."

There was at that time in Jerusalem a holy old man named Simeon. He had set his heart on seeing the Messias who was expected, and had received a promise from the Holy Ghost that this desire should be granted before his own death. While St. Joseph and Our Lady were in the Temple, holy Simeon came in and saw them; and he knew at once that the holy Child whom he saw in the arms of the Queen was the Messias whom the Holy Ghost had promised that he should see. Then

> He also took Him in his arms and blessed God and said: Now dost Thou dismiss Thy servant, O Lord, according to Thy word, in peace; because my eyes have seen Thy salvation which Thou hast prepared before the face of all peoples; a light to the revelation of the gentiles and the glory of Thy people Israel.[1]

While "His father and Mother were wondering at those things which were spoken concerning Him," Simeon blessed them, and told Mary that her Son "was set for the fall and the resurrection of many in Israel, and for a sign that shall be contradicted;" and he added, "And thy own soul a sword shall pierce."[2]

This prophecy of holy Simeon is said to be the First Dolor—or Sorrow—of the Queen, and the sword entered her soul then, for she saw that her divine Son was to have a life of suffering.

A holy widow named Anna who lived in the Temple also knew from the Holy Ghost that the little Babe in Mary's arms was the Messias, and she "confessed to the Lord, and spoke of Him to all who looked for the redemption of Israel."[3]

It is on the feast of the Purification that the ceremony called the Blessing of the Candles takes place throughout the Church. All of the wax candles that are to be used on the altar during the year (or as many as can be obtained) are brought to the sanctuary on the eve or on the morning of the feast, and arranged on a

---

1 Luke 2: 28-32. 2 *Ibid.*, 33-35. 3 *Ibid.*, 38.

side table before holy Mass, together with those which are to be distributed to the people. The priest comes out of the sacristy wearing a purple cope and blesses the candles, reading over them some very beautiful prayers, which you may find in the Missal before the Mass of the feast. He sprinkles the candles three times with holy water, and incenses them.

Then all the people in the church come up to the rails and the priest gives a candle to each one, while the choir sings the canticle of holy Simeon, which you saw on the previous page. When you receive your candle, you must remember to take it in your right hand and kiss it, along with the hand of the priest who gives it. The candles are all lighted before the Gospel and put out before the Creed. They are lighted again before the Elevation in the Mass, and held until after the priest's communion.

But what is the meaning of it all? Why do people carry candles on the feast of the Purification?

The meaning of it is:

First: To remind us that the Son of God is the true Light of the World and that on this day He was carried to the Temple and offered to His eternal Father.

Second: To remind us of the words of holy Simeon, "Now my eyes have seen the Light which is to enlighten all nations."

Third: To remind us of the words of Our Lord: "Let your light shine before all men, that they may see your good works and glorify your Father who is in heaven."[1]

---
1 Matthew 5:16.

Pious persons keep a blessed candle always in the house because it is a devout custom in the Church to place one lighted in the hands of the dying as a sign or symbol of faith.

Where it can be done—especially before Solemn High Mass—after the candles have been blessed and distributed, all the clergy walk in grand procession round the church, carrying their lighted candles in their hands.

You must never make playthings of your blessed candles, nor treat them with disrespect. They are *sacramentals*, and are holy things because they have been made holy by the solemn blessing of the Church. Also, every one who receives a candle on the feast of the Purification should make a donation to pay for it.

The feast of the Purification is a Double, and has a very beautiful Mass of its own. It was kept in the Church in very early ages, but after a while people became remiss and forgot it. But in the year 541, the world was visited by a terrible plague. Nearly all the people of Egypt are said to have died, and the cities of other provinces lost all their inhabitants. The Emperor Justinian, who then ruled at Constantinople, was a very pious man—after a fashion of his own—and he ordered everybody throughout the Roman Empire to keep the feast of the Purification in honor of the Mother of God. This was done, and the plague ceased. The procession was added a little later.

Et adduxit arcam Dei de domo Obededom .. II Reg. 6.

Tu gloria Jerusalem, tu lætitia Israël, tu hon... Jud. 15.

Chapter XIII

The Assumption of the Blessed Virgin Mary

August 15

THE Church keeps no festival in honor of any event in the life of the Queen after the Purification, unless we consider that of the Seven Dolors as such. The Sorrows of Mary are commemorated on two days—the Friday in Passion Week and the third Sunday of September. I will tell you of both together when we come to the Queen's Sundays.

Now we will speak of the Assumption of Our Lady into heaven, which is kept, as you know, on the 15th of August, and is a Holiday—Holy Day—of Obligation; that is, it is one of those days which the Church commands us to keep holy as we keep the Sundays, by hearing Mass and doing no unnecessary servile work.

You know that the Gospels tell us very little about Our Lady during the public life of her divine Son, and nothing at all of what she did or where she lived after His ascension into heaven. Even St. Luke, who loved to write about the holy Child and His Mother, and who also wrote the Acts of the Apostles, tells us nothing at all of what we should so much like to know. We can only suppose that the Queen in her humility desired both St. John and St. Luke to be silent as to all that concerned her. She knew that "henceforth all generations should call her blessed," because "He that is mighty had done great things to her," and that was enough.

But the Apostles and the early Christians treasured many memories of what happened to their Mother and ours; and these memories were handed down in the Church by tradition, even if they were not found in the written word of God. We know that Our Lord when dying left His Blessed Mother to the care of St. John and "That disciple took her to his own."[1]

We learn from tradition that Mary went with her adopted son to Ephesus, and that after spending some years there she returned to Jerusalem in order to visit again the scenes of Our Lord's Passion and death before she herself went to rejoin Him in heaven.

About twelve years after He had ascended from the top of Mt. Olivet her call came, and Mary gave her blessed soul into the hands of God. Her body was buried by the Apostles, but it was not allowed to remain in the tomb. As Our Lord had preserved her soul from the taint of Original Sin, so He preserved

---
1 John 19:27.

her most pure body from the corruption which is a part of sin's punishment. On the third day Mary's soul and body were reunited by the power of God, and borne by angels triumphantly to heaven. This is what is meant by the Assumption.

"Then it is just the same as the Ascension?"

No; it is not at all the same. To ascend is to *go* up by your own will and your own power; to take yourself up, in fact. To be assumed is to *be taken* up by the will and power of another. Our Lord *ascended*—went up—entirely by His own power; the Queen *was assumed* or carried up by the will and power of God.

Two other persons have been assumed into heaven by the power of God: Enoch and Elias.[1] But they were not taken into the heaven of the Beatific Vision, and they must return to earth some day to die. The Blessed Mother's body, on the other hand, was reunited to her soul and passed into the presence of God, where she will be happy for all eternity.

If you look at a picture or a stained-glass window of the Assumption, you will probably see the Apostles represented as kneeling or standing around an open tomb which is filled with flowers—generally roses and lilies. The story is this:

When the Queen was about to die, the Apostles, who had known and loved her, were scattered abroad, "teaching all nations and baptizing them,"[2] but they

---

[1] Their stories may be found briefly told in Genesis 5:21-24 and in 2 Kings 2:8-12, respectively.
[2] Matthew 28:19.

learned by revelation that Mary was leaving the earth, and they were carried by the power of God to Jerusalem that they might see her once more and say farewell. Only poor Thomas was dilatory and came late. (There is somebody—a very kind somebody—who thinks that you may not understand that rather long word, *dilatory*. Well, it means: not prompt; slow to set about doing the right thing.) Thomas did not reach the Holy City until after the burial of the Queen. He was so sorry, and the others were so sorry for him, that they determined to open the sepulcher so that Thomas might look upon the beautiful face once more. But he was really too late this time. "The stone was rolled back from the sepulcher," and they found nothing within but lilies and roses. The body of the Blessed Mother had been taken to heaven.

The Assumption of Our Lady has never been declared an Article of Faith, but has always been believed by the faithful. The Church has testified her approval of the belief by establishing a festival in honor of this great privilege of Mary, and by making this festival a Holy Day of Obligation. It is a Double with an Octave and has its own most beautiful Mass.

The priest wears white vestments on the feast of the Assumption, as on all the festivals of the Queen. Its eve or Vigil is a fasting-day.

The feast of the Assumption has been kept from very early days, but before the invention of printing and telegraphy and such aids to quick learning, knowledge spread slowly. In the fifth century after Our Lord, the Empress Pulcheria,[1] who was a learned lady and a saint besides, sent to the Patriarch of Jerusalem for relics of the Queen, wherewith to enrich a church built in her honor. What the good Patriarch told Pulcheria about the Assumption was the first she had heard of it. However, she took care to let other people know, and very soon the festival of the Assumption was kept throughout the Church.

If ever you go to the Holy Land, you may visit the empty tomb of the Blessed Mother in the Garden of Gethsemane.

---

[1] St Aelia Pulcheria (398/399 to 453 A.D.) also defended Mary as Theotokos against Nestorianism at the councils of Ephesus and Chalcedon.

Part III

Festivals of the Queen's Titles

Part III

Festivals of the Queen's Titles

O far we have been studying the festivals which commemorate events in the life of the Queen. There are others that have been instituted to honor in a particular manner some act of clemency, some special grace, or some apparition of the glorious Mother of God.

If we were to take all the festivals that have been instituted in honor of the many titles of the Queen at all times and for all places, the story would fill a very large book indeed—and this has to be a little one to suit the age and size of those for whom it is written. There was a time when every town and even village had its patronal feast of Our Lady, and some of the Religious Orders had several, no doubt. But some are observed throughout the Church, and have been kept for at least a number of years, as you will find by looking through the Catholic Calendar, or the list of festivals in the Missal or Vespers book. Devotion to Our Lady under four of her titles—Our Lady of

Lourdes, Our Lady of Good Counsel, Our Lady of Perpetual Succour and Our Lady of Fatima—has been spread through the Church only during the past century or two, and although feasts under each of the four titles have been established, their observance is, I think, permitted rather than commanded as yet. But these devotions have spread rapidly, so we will speak of their festivals when we have been through those which are found in the Calendar.

Fecit et altare thymiamatis de lignis setim. Exod. 37, 25.

Urna aurea, habens manna, et virga Aaron. Hebr. 9, 4.

Chapter XIII

Our Lady Help of Christians

May 24

"Almighty and most merciful God, Who for the defense of the Christian people, hast in a marvelous manner raised up a perpetual succour in the most Blessed Virgin Mary; of Thy goodness grant that we, being defended by her powerful protection during the warfare of this life, may be enabled to gain the victory over our malignant enemy in death." —Collect for Feast.

YOU must know, children, that in all ages the Church of God has had *enemies*—that is, those who have hated her and have wished to do her all the mischief that could possibly be done. Satan, of course, is the greatest and worst of all her enemies, but he cannot do much by himself. In order to work any harm to the Church of God he must get people—either her own children or strangers—to do the work for him.

This sort of mischief may be achieved in two ways. First, pagans and infidels can persecute the faithful, deprive them of their property, their liberty, and sometimes even of their life, as the Romans did in the early Church—or they can fight against Christian countries, as Muhammad did in the early ages, and as his followers have continued to do. Secondly, persons can harm the faithful by teaching false doctrines or by denying that the Catholic religion is the true one, as Luther did.

Many years ago there lived a man whose name was Napoleon Bonaparte. He was a Catholic and made his first communion just as you have. There are people who believe that he was really in earnest and loved Our Lord then.

He was sent to a military school in France, and as he was very clever indeed, and tried with all his might to learn what he was taught and to do as he was told, he became a fine soldier and knew exactly how to tell other soldiers what to do. By degrees he rose from one grade to another until at last he was made Commander of the French Armies—he who had once been looked upon as just the poor orphan son of a lawyer in the Island of Corsica.

France was in a bad state just then. The people had cut off the heads of their king and queen, and of hundreds of other persons besides. They had driven away all the priests and Religious whom they had not put to death, and were grown weary of bloodshed at last, and wished to be quiet again. But they were without a leader and did not know what to do next. Then Napoleon saw his opportunity. He knew that *he* was a leader, and persuaded the French people to think so too, until at last they chose him to be their Emperor, and so the little Corsican became the ruler of France.

He was not stupid by any means, and he saw that if the country were to come to any good, the priests must be brought back and the churches which had been closed re-opened. And all this he did.

But his great fortune had turned his head. He was master of France and he wished to be master of the world, so he made war on one country after another and conquered them until nearly everybody was doing just as he wished.

At that time the Pope was ruler of a portion of Italy called the Papal States, and Napoleon resolved to take these States for himself. He ordered Pope Pius VII to give up the Papal States, and when His Holiness refused to do so—for the States of the Church were not his to give—Napoleon sent his soldiers down to overrun Italy. They actually took the Pope prisoner and kept him in captivity, sometimes in France, sometimes in Italy, from 1809 till 1814—five long years. When the Emperor heard that the Pope had excommunicated him for his evil deeds, he wrote to one of his officers, "Does he think that his excommunication can make the arms drop from the hands of my soldiers?"

During this time, Napoleon sent his soldiers into Russia, where he was utterly defeated, and the arms actually did drop from their hands, for the cold was so intense that the men could not hold their guns. Napoleon himself was obliged to run back to France as fast as he could, and the fear of God—and man— overcame him at last.

During all this sorrowful time the faithful throughout the world had been praying to the Queen of Heaven for the Church and her persecuted Head. And Mary heard their prayers. The rulers of the countries of Europe united against Napoleon, for they were tired of his tyranny. They took Italy and demanded that the Pope should be set free and allowed to return to Rome. Napoleon was obliged to comply and the Holy Father came back to the Eternal City on the 24th of May, 1814. In gratitude to the Queen for his deliverance, Pius VII instituted the Feast of Our Lady Help of Christians, and ordered it to be observed throughout the Church on that day.

The feast is a Double with First and Second Vespers, but has no Octave.

Chapter XIV

Our Lady of Mount Carmel

July 16

"Be mindful, O Virgin Mother, to speak good things for us in the sight of God, and to turn away His anger from us."
—Offertory for Feast.

F you look at the map of the Holy Land, children, you will find that it is bounded on the western side by that part of the Mediterranean Sea which is called the *Levant*. Now, begin at the very north and go down the coast. Very soon you will come to a tiny bay—the only bay on the coast of Palestine—and at the south of this bay is Mt. Carmel.

Do you know anything about the prophets Samuel and Elias?

Samuel lived in the time of Saul; Elias was somewhat later. Yet even in their day, there was a kind of convent on Mt. Carmel, and the "Sons of the Prophets"—that is, the pupils and disciples of those holy men—lived and

The Holy Land
at the time of Christ

prayed and studied together there. Tradition declares that, although they are not mentioned in the holy Gospels, the mountain was never without its solitaries who spent their lives in praising God.

During the persecutions of the early Church many Christians took refuge on Mt. Carmel, and by degrees a community was formed; and the Religious who dwelt there were called *Carmelites*. They led very hard lives, sleeping little, but praying and fasting much. Their habit was rough and coarse and the outer part of it was made of a piece of woolen stuff with a hole in the middle so that the head could be put through. This piece of cloth was called a *scapular*, from a Latin word which means shoulders, and it reached nearly to the hem of the monks' gowns (or *habits*) before and behind.

During the Crusades, a number of English Crusaders invited some of the monks of Mt. Carmel to come with them to England, which they did, and the Crusaders helped the Religious to build a large monastery not far from Cambridge, where the great university is now. These Carmelites—for so they were still called—were joined by many novices, and in a short time their convent became celebrated for the sanctity of its inmates.

England was a Catholic country in those days, and many of her children lived very holy lives. Especially were they distinguished for their great love for the Queen. One man named Simeon had betaken himself into a forest at Newnham, near Cambridge, and there he lived a hermit's life in the trunk—or *stock*—of a great hollow tree. So the people, who soon found him out, called him Simon Stock.

When Simon heard of the holy men who had come to live in the forest not far off, he asked to be received among them, and in course of time he became the General of the Carmelite Order.

It happened that when Simon was nearly a hundred years old, on the 16th of July, 1251, he was praying in the chapel at Newnham and begging Our Lady to give him some sign whereby all might know that she was the Lady and Patroness of the Order. His prayer was something like this (only he probably said it in Latin):

> Fair Flower of Mount Carmel! True blossoming rod!
> Bright Splendor of Heaven! Chaste Mother of God!
> With none like to thee!
>
> Meek Mother! Pure Virgin! Bestow from above
> On thy children of Carmel some sign of thy love,
> Clear Star of the Sea!

Then the Queen of Heaven appeared to him, holding in her hand the scapular of the Order, and she said: "This shall be a sign of my favor to thee and to all Carmelites. Whosoever shall die wearing my scapular shall not burn forever in the fires of hell."

With the assurance of this promise, the Confraternity of the Brown Scapular was later instituted, as some believe, by St. Simon Stock himself.

We must not stay now to talk of the devotion of the scapular. You will be enrolled some day, if you do

not already wear the scapular, and then you will learn all about it.

The feast of Our Lady of Mt. Carmel was first kept by the Religious of the Carmelite Order, but is now observed throughout the Church. It is a Double with First and Second Vespers, and has a beautiful Mass of its own, but is kept without an Octave.

Chapter XV

The Blessed Virgin Mary ad Nives, or of the Snow

August 5

"Hail, thou Star of Ocean, Portal of the Sky!
Ever Virgin Mother of the Lord most high!"
—Hymn for Vespers of Feast.

HIS is a festival instituted in order to commemorate the dedication of a very special church in honor of the Queen of Heaven. This Church stands on one of the Seven Hills on which Rome is built, and is known by many names, one of which, Our Lady of the Snow, gives its title to this festival of the Queen.

It happened about the middle of the fourth century—that is, about 350 AD—that there lived in Rome a rich nobleman named John, and his wife, who was rich, noble, and good like himself. They had no children and wished very much to expend their great wealth in honor of the Mother of God, but they could not decide on what she would like best. They prayed very earnestly to God and Our Lady that she would make known her will, and on the night of the 4th of August the Blessed Mother appeared in a dream to each of her devoted servants and told them that she wished them to erect a church in her honor on the Esquiline Hill. They would learn the exact spot whereon it was to be built by visiting the Hill, where they would find a certain piece of ground covered with snow.

In the morning each of these two good people told the other the dream; but as we are taught not to put faith in dreams generally, they did not go off at once to the Esquiline Hill, but went instead to consult a spiritual director, who happened to be Pope Liberius. Then they learned that the Blessed Mother had appeared to him also, and had told him just what she had told them.

The Holy Father with John and his wife visited the spot on the Esquiline Hill which Our Lady had chosen, and there they found that a shower of snow had indeed fallen and covered just so much ground as would serve to build a very large church upon. All the rest of the Hill lay bare under the August sunshine, and they saw at once that Mary had kept her word.

The good Roman and his pious wife, with the help of Pope Liberius, fulfilled the command of the Queen, and built a magnificent church on the spot which they had seen covered by the miraculous fall of snow. It was so magnificent that it was, and still is, often called *Santa Maria Maggiore* or St. Mary Major—that is, the great

The Blessed Virgin Mary ad Nives, or of the Snow

Church of Our Lady. Sometimes, too, it is known as *Santa Maria ad Praesepe*, or St. Mary's of the Crib, because the manger in which the Queen laid the holy Child in the stable at Bethlehem was brought from the Holy Land and placed in this church, where it is still venerated.

But the name which the Romans love best is Our Lady of the Snow, and the memory of the miracle is kept alive in the Holy City in very pretty fashion.

During holy Mass on the morning of the 5th of August white jessamine flowers are showered down from the roof of the church to represent the snowflakes which once covered its site on that day; and the jessamine shower goes on until the feast is over.

There is another precious relic in the Church of Our Lady of the Snow, besides the holy manger, and that is a picture of Mary which is believed to have been painted by St. Luke. The people love this picture very much, and with good reason. Here is that story:

Once, when St. Gregory the Great was Pope, Rome was visited by a terrible plague. Hundreds, perhaps thousands of persons, died; and the survivors were so terrified that many left the city, and those who could not go away were afraid to nurse the sick or to bury the dead.

The saintly Pontiff did all that lay in his power to help the sufferers, but the plague grew worse instead of better, and at last he ordered all who were well enough to join in a grand procession. Then he led his people through the streets singing the great litanies and carrying the picture which is said to have been painted by St. Luke.

Rome stands on the banks of a river called the Tiber, and the great tomb of the Roman Emperor Hadrian sits upon its banks, with a bridge crossing the river at its feet. As the procession reached the head of this bridge, numbers of angels were  heard singing the antiphon which you hear sung after Vespers on the Sundays in Easter time:

> *Regina coeli laetare,*
> *Quia quem meruisti portare,*
> *Resurrexit sicut dixit.*

(That is, in English:)

> Rejoice, O Queen of Heaven, to see
> The Sacred Infant born of thee
> Return in glory from the tomb.

Then St. Gregory sang:

> *Ora pro nobis Deum.*

(in English:)

> Pray for us to God.

Now, as the Pope sang, he saw, standing on the top of Hadrian's Tomb, the glorious Archangel Michael in the act of putting a sword into its sheath to show that the plague was ended, as indeed it really was. Because of this miraculous vision, Hadrian's Tomb was ever after called *Castel Sant' Angelo* and a great bronze statue of St. Michael still stands upon it in memory of this day.

Tradition tells us that this was when and how the *Regina Coeli* was first sung.

Do you wonder that the Roman people love the picture that was carried that day, and feel sure that it was painted by St. Luke?

The feast of *Santa Maria ad Nives* is a Double without an Octave, and the Mass said is that of Our Lady from Pentecost to Advent.

Of course the feast was first kept in Rome—in the Church variously called *Santa Maria ad Nives*—*Santa Maria Maggiore*—*Santa Maria ad Praesepe*. I cannot tell you when this festival was first observed throughout the Church, nor is it of any great consequence. But in future, when you see snow falling, let it remind you of your Mother in heaven as well as of snowballs and sleighing.

Chapter XVI

The Blessed Virgin Mary of Mercy

September 24

"O God, Who, for the deliverance of Christ's faithful people from the hands of the infidels, wast pleased through the most glorious Mother of Thy Son, to enlarge Thy Church with a fresh progeny; grant, we beseech Thee, that as we venerate in her the foundress of so great a work, so by her merits and intercession we may be delivered from all our sins, and from the bondage of the devil." —Collect of Mass for the Feast.

IN the beginning of the seventh century after Our Lord, there lived in Arabia a man named Muhammad, who said he was descended from Ismael the son of Abraham and Agar. Muhammad was very ambitious and very clever, although he could neither read nor write. He took it into his head to found a new religion, which he called *Islam*, in which he denied Our Lord to be the Son of God and taught many other very wicked falsehoods. He gathered numbers of followers and told them that they must fight against all Christians—and pagans also—and compel the people whom they conquered either to embrace his doctrines or to suffer death. The followers of his religion, called *Muslims*, were very strong and very determined. In less than a hundred years they conquered all the countries on the eastern and southern shores of the Mediterranean Sea, and took possession of nearly all the islands in the Levant, as well as most of Spain.

Then they built great ships—the finest in the world at that time, and went up and down the Mediterranean chasing all Christian vessels, seizing them when they could, and ravaging the cities on the shores of Italy and Greece.

All the Christians who fell into the hands of these infidels were carried off to be sold as slaves, and their sufferings were so terrible that hundreds died every year from the hardships they endured. Moreover, many of these poor Christians were weak enough to give up the faith and become Muslims rather than face slavery or certain death. This was the state of affairs at the beginning of the thirteenth century, when Our Lady appeared to each of three of her most devoted servants—St. Peter Nolasco, St. Raymond Pennafort, and James, King of Aragon. She told St. Peter Nolasco, who was a Spanish nobleman, that she wished him to found an Order of Religious Knights who would devote their lives and all that they had to the redemption of Christians taken captive by the Moors.

The Blessed Virgin Mary of Mercy

The next morning Peter went to confession to St. Raymond Pennafort, and told him of the apparition of the Queen; whereupon he learned that the holy priest had also been favored with a visit from the Mother of God, who had told him of her wish too. King James came shortly after with the same story, and the three gentlemen resolved at once to obey the command of the Queen.

The Order was founded under the name of *Our Lady of Mercy for the Redemption of Captives*, and the members bound themselves by vow to devote their lives to the protection of Christians, and more especially to ransoming such as were taken and held in slavery by the Moors. They even vowed to offer themselves in exchange for any whom they could ransom in no other way.

Commonly known as the Mercedarians, their order was approved by Pope Gregory IX and St. Peter Nolasco became its first General Superior. It was by the members of this Order that the Feast of Our Lady of Mercy was first kept. Soon it was observed by all the Spaniards, then by the French; and finally, in the seventeenth century Pope Innocent XII commanded that it should be kept throughout the universal Church on the 24th of September.

The feast of Our Lady of Mercy, also commonly known as Our Lady of Ransom, is a Double. The Mass said is that called *Salve sancta parens*, which takes its name from the first words of the *Introit*. This is the Mass of Our Lady from Easter to Pentecost. The Collect at the head of this chapter belongs especially to the feast.

Chapter XVII

Our Lady of Lourdes

February 11

"I am the Immaculate Conception."
—words of Our Lady to Bernadette.

N the year 1858 there lived at Lourdes, in the south of France, a little girl of fourteen named Bernadette Soubirous. She was the child of very poor parents, and had been sent by her mother to a village not far from Lourdes to be nursed by another poor peasant woman.

Bernadette was very delicate, but her nurse learned to love her dearly, and begged to be allowed to keep the little thing and bring her up with her own children. When the child was old enough, she was allowed to tend a few sheep for her foster parents, but the good people neither sent her to school nor taught her themselves. At fourteen she knew no prayers except the Rosary and had not learned her Catechism nor, of course, made her first communion. She was very ignorant indeed about her religion, and her parents brought her home in order that she might receive instructions for the sacraments.

Of course Bernadette would have been glad to learn had any one offered to teach her, but in spite of her ignorance she had never wilfully told an untruth nor committed an act of disobedience in her life. She loved play, as you do, and wished very much to go into the open air and work in the fields with her sister Marie and the rest of the village children; but her mother allowed none of these things in cold weather because the little girl was not strong.

However, one day—it was on the 11th of February—she was permitted to go out to gather firewood with her sister Marie and another young girl. They reached a brook which had to be crossed, and while Bernadette was preparing to follow her companions, she suddenly saw a most beautiful lady standing in a grotto in the rock which rose on the other side of the stream. She had no idea who it could be, but fell on her knees and said her Rosary. The lady wore a white dress and veil, and a long blue sash was tied about her waist, while a long white rosary hung from her joined hands. She did not speak, and disappeared as Bernadette finished her prayers.

When Bernadette returned home, she told her mother what had happened, but Madame Soubirous did not pay much attention to the story at that time.

However, the child went again and again to the grotto. Sometimes she saw her beautiful lady, sometimes not; but soon the simple country folk believed her tale and many of them went with her and knelt to pray as she did, although no one else ever saw the lady.

Bernadette was told to speak to her lovely visitor, and to sprinkle her with holy water, which she did; but the Queen was not displeased. She only told the child to come nearer because she had a secret to tell her which concerned Bernadette herself alone, and which none other must know. Three such secrets were confided at different times to her little favorite by the Blessed Mother, who also desired her to go to the pastor of the Church at Lourdes, and tell him that the Queen of Heaven wished a sanctuary to be erected in her honor upon that very spot.

Now, the pastors of the Church are too prudent to believe at once all the wonderful things they hear; so the good priest waited.

On the 26th of February, the lady appeared to Bernadette and told her to drink of and wash in the water of the fountain in the grotto—but you can imagine how this confused Bernadette, for there was no fountain in the place. However, the lady repeated her command and pointed to a corner of the grotto, so the little girl knelt down and began to scoop out the dry dust and earth with her hands. Presently a tiny spring began to bubble up, but it was so tiny that the water mixed with the earth and made mud.

Bernadette did not like to put that to her lips. Would you? But the lady told her again to drink and then the little girl took the wet mud and put it into her mouth. It was not at all nice, but the people who were watching and praying came pressing into the grotto, eager to see this wonderful water—and to taste it too. They soon made a deep hole, and the water bubbled up more and more and filled it no matter how much dirt they scooped out.

Soon after this a blind man bathed his eyes in some of the water and his sight was restored. A poor woman put her sick baby into the spring itself. The water was icy cold and the people said the mother was crazy; but they were wrong. The baby was cured.

The villagers of Lourdes had full faith in Bernadette and her beautiful lady; but some clever men thought the child an impostor, others that she dreamed the tales she told. She suffered a great deal of persecution and was even threatened with imprisonment if she persisted in saying that she had seen and spoken with the Blessed Virgin. But Bernadette did not say anything of the kind. She only declared that she saw in the grotto a beautiful lady whom she loved, but whose name she did not know.

At last she resolved to ask the lady herself who she was. On the 25th of March (the feast of the Annunciation, you remember) Bernadette went as usual to the grotto, and presently the lady appeared in her white robe and veil, and with a rose blossoming on each of her shoes. Then Bernadette cried, "Oh, lady, will you have the kindness to tell me your name?" The lady did not answer until the question had been repeated three times, and then she lifted her hands and eyes to heaven and said, "I am the Immaculate Conception."

The Queen appeared several times after that, and the people were determined to build the Church for which she had asked. The tiny spring had gone on flowing and its waters formed a pool in which people could bathe. Many miracles were worked and the fame of the holy place at Lourdes went abroad through the Church.

A magnificent sanctuary was erected upon the rock, and soon thousands of sick people came from all parts to bathe in the miraculous fountain whose waters never ceased to flow. Many, many thousands go there still and such wonderful miracles are performed there that even non-Catholics and infidels have to believe in them. Perhaps you may have the great happiness of making a pilgrimage to Lourdes some day.

Bernadette learned her prayers and her Catechism, made her first communion, and when old enough, became a Sister of Charity at Nevers, a city in France, always remaining as pious, humble, and obedient as when she kept sheep for her foster mother and was looked upon as an ignorant poor girl. She is dead now, and we must hope that she is interceding with the Queen for all of us.

Chapter XVIII

Our Lady of Good Counsel

April 26

"Let us all rejoice in the Lord, celebrating a festival day in honor of the Blessed Virgin Mary, Mother of Good Counsel, at whose solemnity the angels rejoice and give praise to the Son of God. Alleluia. My heart hath uttered a good word: I speak my works to the King." —Introit for Feast.

DO you know the picture of Our Lady of Good Counsel?

"Oh, yes, it is a lovely picture. At least Our Lady is lovely. The holy Child has a bald head."

So He has—and a most beautiful face. After all, a living baby without much hair is not a miracle in nature. Somebody who loved the Queen and her divine Son thought this "the sweetest picture artist ever drew."

You know the hymn to Our Lady of Good Counsel, do you not? The more you look at the picture, the more you will love it. Never mind the bald head. Here is the story of the painting—and of the feast of Our Lady of Good Counsel.

In the middle of the fifteenth century there stood in the town of Genazzano, which is about thirty miles south of Rome, a little old church dedicated to Our Lady of Good Counsel. It was under the care of the Fathers of St. Augustine, and was neither rich nor beautiful.

Now, there lived in the town at that time an old woman named Petruccia, who had a little property. She suddenly declared that she was going to build a fine new church for the Madonna and that a grand lady was coming to live in it. Everybody laughed at old Petruccia and her relations were very angry, because they were afraid that she would spend all her money and then they would have to support her. However, Petruccia cared neither for laughter nor anger. She sold everything she had and the church was begun.

The walls were partly built when the Bishop heard about it—and he began to make inquiries. When he found that a church was being built at Genazzano without permission, by a poor old peasant woman who had very little money, but was persuaded that she had received a revelation (or had a vision—nobody seemed to know which), the Bishop said they must wait.

You see, the bishops and pastors of the Church are not too ready to believe in visions and revelations; more particularly in those of persons who do things without permission from lawful authority. So there was an end, for the present, of Petruccia's church. She stoutly declared that it would yet be built and that the great lady would come to live in it.

The feast of St. Mark was a holiday at Genazzano, and on that day the people always had a fair. The inhabitants of the neighboring villages came into the town, and when the business of the day was over, everybody went to church and then amused themselves for the rest of the evening.

This fair had been held as usual on the 25th of April in the year 1467, and that evening the people were enjoying themselves, each in his own way, when some persons who were standing in the great square of the city saw a curious white cloud floating through the air in the direction of the church. Some of these persons followed the cloud, until presently it settled against one of the walls of poor Petruccia's unfinished sanctuary. Then it seemed to divide and disappear, but where it had rested for a moment was a beautiful picture of Our Lady and the holy Child which had certainly not been there before.

As the cloud vanished, the bells of the church close by—in fact, all the bells of all the churches in the town of Genazzano—began to peal out, and yet nobody rang them. All the people came running to see what had happened—Petruccia, of course, among them. Seeing the picture, she threw herself on her knees before it with arms outstretched, declaring that here was the great lady who was to come and dwell in her new church.

Everybody thought that the Madonna which had come among them so suddenly must have been painted by the angels, and so they called it at once Our Lady of Paradise. It is not painted on wood or canvas, as most pictures are, but on plaster such as you see on the walls of a room sometimes, and this plaster is very thin. Such pictures are often painted on the walls of churches and are called *frescoes;* but they cannot be removed from one place to another, because the plaster would fall to pieces.

The faithful of Genazzano concluded beyond all doubt that the wonderful picture was miraculous. The sick and infirm were brought to pray before it, and nearly all of them were healed, so that the town was very soon crowded with strangers who came to see the marvelous sight.

Then something happened that was almost more marvelous. Two foreigners appeared in Rome, asking about a picture which had disappeared from a church outside Scutari, a city of Albania. (Albania is a little country on the eastern shore of the Adriatic, and Scutari is about twenty miles from the sea.) It was threatened at that time by the Turks, who did shortly afterward invade Albania and put many of the people to death.

The two men who came to Rome soon after that famous feast of St. Mark said that they had been kneeling in prayer before the fresco of the Madonna in the church at Scutari when all at once it became enveloped in a white cloud which rose up and disappeared, carrying the picture with it. The two men followed, and were caught up—they knew not how—and carried after the picture until it vanished and they found themselves standing at the gates of Rome.

But no picture was known to have come to the Eternal City, and it was all in vain that the two Albanians wandered from church to church looking for their beloved Madonna. At the end of two or three days, however, they were told of the wonderful thing that had happened at Genazzano. Straightway they set off for that city, and there they found the picture which they had been seeking hitherto in vain.

The people of Genazzano, who firmly believed that their lovely new Madonna had been painted by angels expressly for them, were not too anxious to accept as truth the testimony of the strangers.

But Pope Paul II sent two bishops to inquire into the story at Genazzano, and another was dispatched to Scutari to examine the little church on the hill whence the picture was said to have disappeared. The good people of Scutari were found in great grief over the loss of a picture of Our Lady which had been held in veneration there for ages, and they showed the place on the wall from which the fresco had apparently been taken away. Everything was found to be exactly as the two men had said. So at last the people of Genazzano who had laughed at poor Petruccia about building her church were glad to be allowed to finish it themselves.

Since then many Cardinals, Bishops, and even Popes have gone on pilgrimages to the Shrine of Our Lady of Good Counsel at Genazzano, and in 1777 the Augustinian Fathers obtained permission to use an Office composed expressly for the feast, which is kept on the 26th of April. It has also its own very beautiful Mass.

Chapter XIX

Our Lady of Perpetual Succour

April 27

THIS will be the story of another picture—one that you probably know well, for copies of it are now to be seen almost everywhere.

It does not strike us as being a very pretty picture when we first look at it. The holy Child is too tall and too old to be carried, and we wonder why He is losing His shoe. Then a little girl was once heard to say that she "could not believe that Our Lady ever had eyes like that." But people who know the picture well learn to love it very dearly, and what is more, the Queen herself appears to love it dearly, too. The original painting is at Rome in a church belonging to the Redemptorist Fathers, on the Esquiline Hill, not far from that of Our Lady of the Snow.

But it was not always there. In the fourteenth century, a gentleman left Crete for fear of the Turks and sought refuge in Rome. He took with him a picture of the Mother of God to which he had a particular devotion and which he called Our Lady of Perpetual Succour. He died at Rome in the house of a friend, and before his departure made his friend promise that after his death the precious picture should be exposed for public veneration in one of the churches of the Eternal City. But the friend was himself so much attached to the painting that despite his promise he could not make up his mind to part with it. Our Lady appeared to him in a dream and warned him that he was bound to keep his word, but he would not heed, and died shortly afterward with the picture still in his house.

The widow of this man valued the picture even more than her husband had done and would not give it up until her little daughter assured her that a beautiful lady told her that the picture of Our Lady of Perpetual Succour must be set up in one of the churches in Rome. Then at last the woman resolved to obey; but just as she was going to have the picture removed, a friend came in who laughed at the idea of giving it up. She even mocked at and spoke disrespectfully of the Queen of Heaven. But the unfortunate creature was stricken there and then with a dangerous illness and was cured only after begging pardon of the Mother of God and asking permission to touch the picture.

Then at last Our Lady was placed in an old church dedicated to St. Matthew. This church belonged to the Augustinian Fathers and stood on the Esquiline Hill;

for the Blessed Mother had declared her wish to dwell on that Hill and in some place not far distant from Santa Maria ad Nives.

Here the picture remained for three hundred years, and many miracles were wrought during that time in favor of persons who invoked the intercession of the Queen before the shrine that she evidently loved. The picture came to be known by the people of Rome as "The Miraculous Madonna."

When the French armies under Napoleon took possession of Rome, the Augustinians were driven from their convent, which was turned into a barracks, and they took the picture with them to their new abode. They were afraid to expose their treasure to the veneration of the faithful, lest it should be stolen like everything else, so they hung it in a little side chapel and its existence was, in a few years, almost forgotten.

But Our Lady had not forgotten it. An old Augustinian lay brother who knew the whole story often used to tell it to a lad named Michael Marchi who, when he grew up, became a Redemptorist—a member, that is, of the Congregation of the Most Holy Redeemer, founded by St. Alphonsus Ligouri.

In 1854 the Redemptorist Fathers bought the site of that old church of St. Matthew wherein Our Lady of Perpetual Succour had been first exposed to the veneration of the devout. They built a church and convent here and Michael Marchi, now a priest of the Order, remembered the Madonna of Brother Orsetti and told the story to his superiors. The Father General asked permission from the Pope to take possession of the long-forgotten picture, and Our Lady returned to her old home on the Esquiline Hill. This did not happen, however, until 1866. On the 23rd of June, 1867, the holy picture was solemnly crowned with a diadem of gold and precious stones. The stories of miracles worked by the intercession of Our Lady of Perpetual Succour would fill a volume.

As for why the Holy Child is losing his shoe…well, if you notice, at the top of the picture there are two angels. These are the Archangels Michael and Gabriel, holding the instruments of Christ's Passion. It is said that as our infant Lord beholds these cruel instruments, his anguish is so great that, in his hurry to fly to his mother's comforting arms, he has lost his shoe.

You know that *perpetual succour* means help that goes on always—help at all times and under all circumstances. So you may go to Our Lady of Perpetual Succour and tell her what you want, just as you go to your mother here below.

Chapter XX

Our Lady of Fatima

May 13

IN THE tiny hamlet of Aljustrel, a mile south of the village of Fatima in Portugal, lived three children: Francisco and Jacinta Marto, and their cousin who lived nearby, Lucia dos Santos, who was the youngest of seven, but preferred her cousins as playmates. These three children were frolicking in the fields one day in the spring of 1916, pasturing their sheep, when suddenly a strong gust of wind blew through the trees and they saw a bright light descending toward them. As it came closer, they saw that this light came from a young man who shone from within.

"Fear not! I am the Angel of Peace," he said to them. "Pray with me." Kneeling on the ground in supplication, he thrice repeated this prayer:

> My God, I believe, I adore, I hope and I love You. I beg pardon of You for those who do not believe, do not adore, do not hope and do not love You.

Three times the Angel of Peace visited the children, each time urging them to pray and offer reparation to God for all the offenses of mankind. And though they obeyed the angel and prayed, they were not sure how to explain to their families the visits of this beautiful stranger, so they said nothing.

And I am sorry to say it, but like many young children, their method of praying was not very diligent (that means careful). Lucia was but 9 years old, Francisco 8 and Jacinta 6. So perhaps you will not be surprised to hear their shortcut for saying the Rosary. Instead of reciting each prayer in full, they said only the first words of each: "Our Father" and then ten times "Hail Mary," followed by "Glory be to the Father,"—and with marvelous speed, one decade was done!

They had just finished praying in this way one Sunday morning—it was the thirteenth of May, 1917, a year or so after they had first been visited by the Angel—when a flash like lightning startled the children. Thinking a storm was coming, they hastened to collect their flock and hurry home, when an even brighter flash stopped them in their tracks. There before them, hovering just above the branches of a small tree, was the most beautiful lady they had ever seen, dressed all in white and sparkling like the sun shining through crystal. Her hands were folded in prayer upon her breast, and she held a Rosary with beads like stars. Yet her eyes looked so serious—almost sad.

"Don't be afraid," she said to them in a sweet-sounding voice, "I will do you no harm."

Curious, Lucia asked the lady, "Where do you come from?"

"I come from heaven," was the answer.

"And what do you want of me?" Lucia wondered.

"I want you to come to this place for the next six months, on the thirteenth of each month, at the same hour. Then I will tell you who I am and what I desire."

Emboldened, Lucia asked the lady, "And shall I go to heaven?"

"Yes, you will."

"And Jacinta?"

"Also."

"What about Francisco?"

The Lady gazed at Francisco with a serious look. "He too, but he will have to say many Rosaries first."

(Sadly, though Francisco was enraptured with the sight of this beautiful lady, he could not hear her words.)

Lucia then asked the heavenly lady about two friends of her family that had recently died. She was surprised to learn that while one was in heaven, the other would remain in Purgatory until the end of the world! This thought weighed heavily upon her.

Then the lady spoke once more: "Are you willing to offer yourselves to God, and endure whatever suffering He may send you, in order to make reparation to him for all the sins that offend Him, and for the conversion of sinners?"

"Yes! We will!" Lucia cried.

"Then you shall have much to suffer. But the grace of God will help you to endure." And as the lady spoke these words, she extended her hands, from which shone forth beams of light that seemed to penetrate deep into their souls and fill them with the promised grace. They fell to their knees and prayed.

Now the lady spoke once more, admonishing the children, "Pray the Rosary every day, that you may obtain peace for the world and an end to the war." For a great and terrible war was then raging through the whole of Europe. Having said this, she began to float upwards and away toward the east, leaving the children to gaze after her lovingly until she disappeared from sight.

And the lady's prediction came true, for though they were faithful to their promise to return on the thirteenth of each month, they had much to suffer in doing so, with the resistance of their parents and even the government of Portugal, which was controlled by men who did not believe in God and hated the Church. They suspected the priests of conjuring up this tale with the children to gain money and fame. They even tried locking the children up in jail to prevent them from going to the Cova da Iria (the place where the apparations had taken place) and they tried to force them to reveal the secrets the lady had entrusted to their care. But though the children were frightened and lonely, nothing could make them alter their story, nor share what the lady had told them in secret, and they offered their sufferings to Jesus for the conversion of sinners.

When the lady appeared in July, she showed the children a vision of the souls suffering in hell. This vision was so terrifying that Lucia later said they would likely have died of fright, had they not felt safe in the presence of the Mother of God, and her promise that they should go to heaven.

The lady told them, "You have seen Hell, where the souls of poor sinners go. To save them, God wishes to establish throughout the world devotion to my Immaculate Heart. If people will do what I ask, many souls will be saved and there will be peace." The lady predicted that the war would end soon, but that another more terrible war would come if people continued to offend God. To prevent this, she asked that Russia be consecrated to her Immaculate Heart, lest that country's errors be spread throughout the world and bring much suffering and persecution of the Church. But she promised them that despite all, in the end, her Immaculate Heart would triumph. She then taught them to say the following prayer after each decade of the Rosary:

> Oh my Jesus, forgive us our sins, save us from the fires of Hell. Lead all souls to heaven, especially those in most need of Thy mercy.

Many flocked to the site of the apparitions in the hopes of seeing even the just the shadow of the lady's presence, or of hearing the soft hum of her voice, like that of a bee, even though her words could not be made out. But there were many who either doubted or even held such faith in scorn. To convince all, the lady promised to perform a great miracle during her apparition in October.

Believers and unbelievers alike gathered from far and near at the appointed time, to behold either a miracle, or proof that these children were impostors. Rain soaked the fields where men, women and children encamped in the mud through the night, that they might be present for this sign from heaven. Many prayed for the healing of a loved one while shivering in the damp, cold night. Rumors passed around that great harm might come to the children should the promised miracle fail to take place. Amid this dreary scene, the weak grey light of dawn found 70,000 people waiting, praying the Rosary and singing hymns.

The long-awaited moment arrived and the lady kept her promise, revealing to the children, "I am the Lady of the Rosary. I have come to warn the faithful to amend their lives and ask pardon for their sins. They must not continue to offend our Lord, who is already so deeply offended. They must say the Rosary. Let them continue saying it every day." She then showed the children St. Joseph and her Divine Son. As she was about to depart, she gestured with her hand toward the sky, prompting Lucia to cry out, "Look at the sun!"

Three times the amazed spectators observed the sun dancing in the sky, shedding rays of many colors in every direction. Then it seemed to plunge toward the earth, inflicting terror in those who stood watching. Many fled for fear that the end of the world was at hand, begging the Mother of God for her protection.

Then as suddenly as it had begun, the sun returned to its place in the sky, leaving the bewildered multitude to gaze in astonishment around them. What twelve minutes ago had been a rainy, muddy quagmire was now dry—right down to the clothing on their backs, which had been sodden to the skin just moments before. Here and there the voice of rejoicing was heard as poor sufferers found themselves or their loved ones healed.

Nor were the occupants of the field the only ones to witness this spectacle, for skeptics and believers alike reported seeing this curious phenomenon as far away as 300 miles. Newspaper reporters who had been on hand—most of them among the scoffers—featured long and detailed accounts of this great Miracle throughout Portugal.

And what became of these three children? The lady had revealed to Lucia that Francisco and Jacinta would come to heaven soon, but that she must remain for a time, so that by means of her witness and intercession, a great devotion to the Immaculate Heart of Mary might be established. This indeed came to pass, for a terrible epidemic of influenza passed over Europe soon after, and after much patient suffering, Our Lady came as promised to bring the two little ones home to heaven. Lucia entered the religious life when she was old enough, and in 1928 a great basilica finally began to rise from the lowly Cova da Iria, as the Lady had requested.

Part IV

The Queen's Sundays

Chapter XXI

The Feast of the Most Holy Name of Mary

"Through Thy mercy, O Lord, and by the intercession of Blessed Mary ever Virgin, may this oblation procure for us perpetual prosperity and peace." —Secret of Mass for Feast.

ESIDES her other festivals, two Sundays in September and all the Sundays in October are dedicated in honor of the Queen. The first of these is the Sunday within the Octave of her Nativity, when we celebrate the feast of her Most Holy Name. We spoke of this feast earlier, in Chapter VI, but we mention it again here, as it is one of the Queen's Sundays as well.

This festival in honor of the Queen was instituted by Pope Innocent XI to commemorate a victory gained over the infidels through the intercession of Mary. In 1683 the Turks had overrun a great part of Europe and their armies actually reached Vienna and laid siege to that great city.

Vienna is the capital of Austria, and if you look for it on the map, you will find it almost in the center of Europe—that is, the center of the Christian world at that time. Had Vienna fallen into the hands of the Turks, as almost every one feared that it must, the consequences to the Church would have been terrible.

The emperor of Austria—he was called emperor of Germany then—was vain, conceited, and a great coward. Instead of trying to defend his people and his capital, he lost heart and ran away, leaving the Viennese to do the best they could.

When all the food stored up in the city was exhausted, no more could be had; for the Turks had set up their camp all round the city so that no one could get in with supplies and the soldiers and others could obtain nothing for themselves, or for the women and children who were shut up with them within the walls.

They ate up dogs, cats, horses—even their own boots. The king of France hated the Germans and would not help them; and everybody was afraid of the Turks.

A very brave and noble gentleman named John Sobieski had been chosen by the people of Poland to be their king, and when he heard that the Turks had besieged Vienna, he called his soldiers together and set off on the feast of Our Lady's Assumption to help his fellow Christians in their need. He managed to climb up a steep mountain with his troops so that the infidels should not know that he was there, and on September 12—the Sunday within the Octave of the Nativity of

Mary—he rushed down upon the Turkish camp and drove the Muslim invaders away.

Vienna was saved—perhaps all Europe—and while everybody was praising John Sobieski, he gave all the honor and glory of his victory to the ever blessed Mother of God.

He was treated very badly by the Emperor, who was jealous of the brave warrior and angry because Sobieski had saved the city from which he himself had run away.

The feast of the Holy Name of Mary is a Double without an Octave, and has a Mass of its own.

Chapter XXII

The Feast of the Seven Dolors of the Blessed Virgin Mary

Third Sunday of September

"*There stood by the cross of Jesus, Mary His Mother, and His Mother's sister Mary of Cleophas, and Salome, and Mary Magdalen.*

"*Vers.: Woman, behold thy son, said Jesus. To the Disciple however: Behold thy Mother.*" —Introit of Mass for Feast.

HERE are, in reality, *two* days consecrated to the memory of the *Dolors* or Sorrows of the Queen. One is the Friday in Passion Week, when we commemorate most particularly the anguish endured by the ever-blessed Mother while standing at the foot of the cross. During the Mass for this feast, there is a special *sequence* (that is, a hymn that sometimes follows the *gradual*) called the *Stabat Mater* which commemorates those sorrowful hours thus spent. It is very beautiful and you should learn it someday.

This feast was first kept in the diocese of Cologne in the year 1423, and spread thence into many countries. In 1727, Benedict XIII ordered that it should be observed throughout the Church.

The second of these two feasts was first granted in 1668 to the Servites (also called the Servants of Mary), to be celebrated on the third Sunday in September. It was later extended to the whole Church by Pope Pius VII out of gratitude to Our Lady, to whose intercession he attributed his deliverance from captivity under the tyranny of Napoleon (see Chapter XII for that story).

Can you name the seven sorrows of our Lady which we commemorate on these feasts? They are:

1. The Prophecy of Simeon.
2. The Flight into Egypt.
3. The Loss of the Child Jesus in the Temple.
4. The Meeting on the Via Dolorosa.
5. The Crucifixion.
6. The Descent from the Cross.
7. The Burial of Jesus.

It was revealed to St. Bridget of Sweden that these seven signal graces would be bestowed upon those who pray seven *Hail Marys* while meditating on each of the Seven Sorrows of Mary:

1. I will grant peace to their families.
2. They will be enlightened about the divine mysteries.
3. I will console them in their pains and I will accompany them in their work.
4. I will give them as much as they ask for as long as it does not oppose the adorable will of my divine Son or the sanctification of their souls.

5. I will defend them in their spiritual battles with the infernal enemy and I will protect them at every instant of their lives.
6. I will visibly help them at the moment of their death, they will see the face of their Mother.
7. I have obtained from my divine Son, that those who propagate this devotion to my tears and dolors, will be taken directly from this earthly life to eternal happiness since all their sins will be forgiven and my Son and I will be their eternal consolation and joy.

Both feast days are Doubles and the same Mass is said on both, and in white vestments.

Chapter XXIII

Feast of the Holy Rosary of the Blessed Virgin Mary

First Sunday of October

"In me is all grace of the way and of Truth: In me is all hope of Life and of Virtue. I have flowered forth like a rose planted by the brooks of water." —Offertory of Mass for Feast.

EFORE the end of the sixteenth century the Turks, who had determined to conquer Europe, as they had already conquered Asia and Africa, had made themselves almost entirely masters of the Mediterranean Sea. They possessed more warships than any other single nation, for although Venice had a very fine navy and built more ships than any other country, she sold many of the ships she built and did not much care what went on in the Mediterranean or elsewhere as long as she could keep the infidels out of the Adriatic, where most of her own possessions were situated.

EUROPE AT THE TIME OF THE BATTLE OF LEPANTO (SHOWN WITH A STAR)

The Turkish fleet, consisting of three hundred vessels, had gathered in the Gulf of Lepanto on the coast of Greece, in the beginning of October 1571. From thence the Sultan Selim II intended to make a descent upon Italy, and to take and probably destroy Rome. The Pope at that time was St. Pius V, and he commanded all Christians throughout the Church to unite in prayer against the infidels. He persuaded the king of Spain, Philip II, to send a fleet, borrowed some ships from the Venetians, who feared for the safety of their own republic, and sent all the Roman galleys to Lepanto under the command of a brave, good man named Don John of Austria. All these vessels put together were very few in comparison with the immense numbers in the Turkish fleet, but all Christendom was praying to Mary, and Don John, trusting in the intercession of the Queen whose servant he was, was not at all afraid.

The battle came off on the first Sunday of October and the Christians gained a glorious victory. Standing at a window of the Vatican Palace, Pope Pius V saw it all—although he was in Rome and the battle was fought far away, off the coast of Greece. Out of gratitude to the Mother of God, Pius V instituted a feast to be kept on the first Sunday in October, and called it the Feast of Our Lady of Victory. His successor, Gregory XIII, changed this name to that of Our Lady of the Rosary.

This festival is a Double, with First and Second Vespers, and the priest wears white vestments at Mass.

The remaining Sundays of October are dedicated in honor of the Maternity, the Purity, and the Patronage of our immaculate Queen.

In the Maternity of Mary we venerate her wonderful privilege of being the Mother of God.

In the festival of her Purity we do special homage to her entire freedom from every stain of sin.

On the feast of her Patronage we invoke her particularly as our beloved Protectress and Advocate.

As Sundays do not fall always on the same day of the month, these feasts become movable and therefore are liable to be transferred or even set aside altogether in favor of some more important festival which may fall on that day of the month. Nevertheless, they belong to the Queen, and she wishes to be particularly invoked and remembered by her children on these Sundays, whether it be possible to say her Mass in public or not.

In 1883, Pope Leo XIII consecrated the whole month of October to Our Lady by commanding that the Rosary be said in public every day; so that this has become in fact a second month of Mary.

Chapter XXIV

The Queen's Month

MAY

"Most Holy Mary, at thy feet We bend a suppliant knee; In this thine own sweet Month of May, Pray thou to God for me."
—Hymn for May.

HE Queen has, in reality, two months—for, as we saw in the previous chapter, October has become hers, and the angels rejoice to share it with her. But the month of May is that which we have been accustomed to think of as the true month of Mary, and we look forward to her processions, the May devotions, and the crowning of her statue, much as we look forward to Easter and Whitsuntide. The Church has not as yet appointed any set form of liturgical devotion for the services of this month. They are left to the choice of the pastor, and most frequently consist of some English prayers—usually a portion of the Rosary and an Act of Consecration, a short lecture, and Benediction. The

statue of Our Lady is, in many churches, crowned on the first Sunday in May, to show that we have chosen her to be *our* Queen as she is the Queen of the angels in heaven.

May is the beautiful month, the month of sunshine and flowers, when earth is really awake after her long winter sleep. People always loved May, even in the old pagan times, and celebrated the coming of the month of blossoms and young leaves with festivals and rejoicings. For hundreds of years after the coming of Our Lord these rejoicings were kept up. The faithful, especially those children of the Church who lived in the country, heard Mass in the morning very early indeed, and then the young folks went off to the woods and meadows to gather flowers and green branches wherewith to deck the Maypole—and themselves. They chose a queen from among the maidens, and she was to be the one of them all who was distinguished for her modesty, piety, and general good behavior.

In the evening she held her Court and there was a dance around the Maypole on the village green.

All this was very charming, and for a long time was very innocent, too. But a time came when holy Mass was set aside, and May brought no thought of anything better than idle enjoyment. Then worse set in, and in the month which bears Mary's name, the Queen was but too often dishonored.

Several hundred years ago, some good pastors who were grieved to see such an abuse determined to do what they could to put an end to it. They led their people in procession in honor of the Mother of God, and taught the young folks and the children to bring their flowers to her, and to crown her—surely the fairest and holiest of all the daughters of men—as their Queen.

Try to keep Mary's Month as well as you can. Bring her flowers, learn to sing her hymns—and be sure to get the words correctly and pronounce them distinctly—and, if you can, do something more than usual for her poorer little ones. Then you will be able to sing with truth to your Mother in heaven the words of Father Faber's beautiful hymn for her month:

> Joy of my heart, O let me pay
> To thee thine own sweet Month of May.[1]

---

1 *Oratory Hymns*, 1860.

Additional titles available from

St. Augustine Academy Press
Books for the Traditional Catholic

Titles by Mother Mary Loyola:

Blessed are they that Mourn
Confession and Communion
Coram Sanctissimo (Before the Most Holy)
First Communion
First Confession
Forgive us our Trespasses
Hail! Full of Grace
Heavenwards
Home for Good
Jesus of Nazareth: The Story of His Life Written for Children
Questions on First Communion
The Child of God: What comes of our Baptism
The Children's Charter
The King of the Golden City
The Little Children's Prayer Book
The Soldier of Christ: Talks before Confirmation
Trust
Welcome! Holy Communion Before and After
With the Church

Titles by Father Lasance:

The Catholic Girl's Guide
The Young Man's Guide

Tales of the Saints:

A Child's Book of Saints by William Canton
A Child's Book of Warriors by William Canton
Legends & Stories of Italy by Amy Steedman
Mary, Help of Christians by Rev. Bonaventure Hammer
Page, Esquire and Knight by Marion Florence Lansing
The Book of Saints and Heroes by Leonora Lang
Saint Patrick: Apostle of Ireland
The Story of St. Elizabeth of Hungary by William Canton

Check our Website for more:
www.staugustineacademypress.com

The Seat of Wisdom Series

Learn the lesser-known traditional teachings of our Faith
An excellent supplement to any catechesis program!

BY MOTHER MARY ST. PETER
of the Society of the Holy Child Jesus
originally published between 1905 and 1910

Mary the Queen:
A Life of the Blessed Mother for her Little Ones

The Lessons of the King:
Parables Made Plain for His Little Ones

Talks with the Little Ones about the Apostle's Creed

The Queen's Festivals:
An Explanation of the Feasts of the Blessed Virgin Mary

The Story of the Friends of Jesus

The Story of the Miracles of Our Lord

The Gift of the King:
A Simple Explanation of the Doctrines & Ceremonies
of the Holy Sacrifice of the Mass

The Laws of the King:
Talks on the Commandments

"The Sisters of the Holy Child in America have made a distinctly valuable contribution to religious literature for children. There are nearly a dozen neatly printed and illustrated volumes...which are, like Mother Loyola's books, a real joy and help to the child."
—The Ecclesiastical Review, July 1910.

"[Mother Mary St. Peter] has a very clear, pleasing style; and she knows youthful hearts thoroughly. Her talks about the Commandments are excellent, not saying too much, and showing a great deal of shrewdness and discretion in her way of putting things. We are sure that the whole series, of which this is the newest volume, must be very useful for those who are responsible for the instruction of the young."
—The Irish Monthly, July 1910.

www.ingramcontent.com/pod-product-compliance
Lightning Source LLC
Chambersburg PA
CBHW032358040426
42451CB00006B/57